How to Stand Against
A Spiritual Attack

David Holdaway

E–mail: davidholdaway1@aol.com

Cover design by Graham Alder

ISBN 978-1-907929-03-8

David Holdaway has been a minister in the Elim Pentecostal Church of Great Britain for over 26 years. He has been married to Jan for 28 years and they have one daughter, Deborah.

Life Publications

*Therefore put on the full armor of God, so that when the day of evil comes, you may be able to **stand** your ground, and after you have done everything, to **stand***

Ephesians 6:13

How to Stand Against a Spiritual Attack

The Lord is my light and my salvation whom shall I fear? The Lord is the stronghold of my life of whom shall I be afraid?

Psalm 27:1-6

Contents

How to Stand Against a Spiritual Attack

Introduction

In December 1941, Japan launched a massive air attack on the American Pacific fleet at Pearl Harbour in Hawaii. Without a declaration of war the Japanese destroyed the naval and military base inflicting terrible destruction and loss of life. The attack has gone down as one of the most infamous acts in military history. The American President, Franklin D. Roosevelt, proclaimed December 7, 1941, "a date which will live in infamy."

Even though the two nations were not at war, American intelligence had warned that the Japanese were preparing something sinister. Tragically, it was either ignored or acted on too late. When it comes to spiritual warfare good intelligence is vital and acting upon it even more so. Our adversary the devil is merciless. He will speak peace yet plan to attack. This is why we are told of his presence and activity so early on in only the third chapter of the Bible, and throughout scripture we are constantly warned of his menace and threat.

The devil's number one priority in a person's life is to stop them loving God with all their heart, mind and soul. He will do everything he can to stop followers of Jesus from becoming fruitful and effective. Like Pharaoh of old (Exodus 1:10) he fears that if these people rise his kingdom will be destroyed.

This book is primarily about defensive spiritual warfare because we need to know how to stand in God before we go storming the powers of darkness. Sadly, there are multitudes of Christians who are casualties of spiritual conflict because even though they sang the songs of battle and quoted the scriptures of warfare they did not know how to stand against a spiritual attack. Many have left the battlefield beaten up and bloodied never to return. Then there are others who are totally ignorant of spiritual warfare who need to wake up and "smell the conflict."

Don't make the mistake of thinking "defensive" and "standing" means being inactive or negative. On the contrary – it means positioning ourselves to win great victories. The devil's power is real but limited and cannot even be compared to God who is almighty. He is an enemy we have to face but not fear.

At the cross Jesus won a total irrevocable victory over the devil and all the powers of hell. The apostle Paul tells us that Christ, *"having disarmed the powers and authorities, He made a public spectacle of them, triumphing over them by the cross,"* Colossians 2:15. The apostle John puts it like this, *"They overcame him (the devil) by the blood of the Lamb and by the word of their testimony."* You can prove this. The next time the devil comes against you, submit to God, stand and resist him in Jesus' name and he will flee from you, James 4:7.

"If God is for us who can be against us?"

1

Prepare For War

Fight the good fight of faith
1 Timothy 6:12

I have a good friend who before her conversion was a witch for many years. She belonged to a coven in the south of England which was very active not only in practicing their "craft" but in desecrating churches and praying against Christians. She told me they had prayer lists in the coven. She was wonderfully saved and had a tremendous deliverance, but before one ministry session voices told her to take a knife to kill the pastor who was going to pray for her. God miraculously intervened and he was protected and she was set free. She told me some years after she became a Christian there was one thing that really bothered her about church. Even though she knew the power of Jesus was far greater than the devil's, those in the coven were far more devoted to what they practiced than many Christians were to what they believed.

One prominent witch made the statement in an interview I saw that there were now as many witches as there were committed Christians in the United Kingdom. She got her facts completely wrong as there are an estimated 30,000 witches and several million born again followers of Christ. But what was interesting was she recognised a difference between those who call themselves Christians and those who are "committed" Christians.

In her book *From Witchcraft to Christ*, Doreen Irving tells how she descended into the depths of witchcraft and satanism and was crowned queen of the black witches in a ceremony on Dartmoor in the south of England. That night she says, she physically saw the devil and walked through a huge bonfire and met him in the centre of it with both walking through it untouched by the flames. Years later, desperately seeking peace and freedom she gave her life to Christ and for the first time discovered a power far greater than anything she had known before. But a few nights after she went forward for salvation at an evangelistic rally in Bristol, England, she described how the devil physically appeared to her in her bedroom and told her she belonged to him and tried to strangle her. When she cried out the name of Jesus Satan fled and she then knew there was a power greater than the darkness that had filled her life. She was later delivered of all her demonic problems and describes how on two occasions when receiving ministry she physically saw Jesus. (I tell the story in far greater detail in my book *They Saw Jesus*).

The great 18th century evangelist and founder of Methodism, John Wesley, records in his *Journal* what he calls "a terrible sight,"

> Returning in the evening, I was exceedingly pressed to go back to a young woman in Kingswood, England, (the fact I nakedly relate and leave every man to his own judgment of it.) She was nineteen or twenty years old, but, it seems, could not write or read. I found her on the bed, two or three persons holding her. It was a terrible sight. Anguish, horror, and despair above

all description appeared in her pale face. The thousand distortions of her whole body showed how the dogs of hell were gnawing her heart. The shrieks intermixed were scarcely to be endured. But her stony eyes could not weep. She screamed out, as soon as words could find their way, 'I am damned, damned; lost forever! Six days ago you might have helped me. But it is past. I am the devil's now. I have given myself to him. His I am. Him I must serve. With him I must go to hell. I will be his. I will serve him. I will go with him to hell. I cannot be saved. I will not be saved. I must, I will, I will be damned!" She then began praying to the devil. We began, (to sing) *Arm of the Lord, awake, awake!'*

She immediately sank down as sleep; but, as soon as we left off, broke out again, with inexpressible vehemence: "Stony hearts, break! I am a warning to you. Break, break, poor stony hearts! Will you not break? What can be done more for stony hearts? I am damned that you may be saved. Now break, now break, poor stony hearts! You need not be damned, though I must." She then fixed her eyes on the corner of the ceiling and said: "There he is: ay, there he is! Come, good devil, come! Take me away. You said you would dash my brains out: come, do it quickly. I am yours. I will be yours. Come just now. Take me away."

We interrupted her by calling again upon God, on which she sank down as before; and another young woman began to roar out as loud as she had done. My brother (Charles) now came in, it

13

being about nine o'clock. We continued in prayer till past eleven, when God in a moment spoke peace into the soul, first of the first tormented, and then of the other. And they both joined in singing praise to Him who had "stilled the enemy and the avenger."

(Four days later) I was sent for to Kingswood again, to one of those who had been so ill before. A violent rain began just as I set out, so that I was thoroughly wet in a few minutes. Just as that time the woman (then three miles off) cried out, "Yonder comes Wesley, galloping as fast as he can."

Before I continue, led me share an experience I once had when praying for a woman who had violent anger and rage problems. We were in the church office and I had with me the assistant minister and another lady who was part of one the church's ministry teams. As we prayed for the woman she became extremely angry and began to demonically manifest. When she calmed down she asked for a glass of water and the assistant pastor went to the kitchen which was some distance away and behind several closed doors, it was impossible to be see or hear anything taking place there. As we waited for his return she began to become very agitated and angry and said, "I am not drinking that water, he is there praying over it." No one there could have known this as it was impossible to see or hear. When he returned the woman threw the water away and when I asked if he had prayed over it in the kitchen he said, yes he had. The demonic powers within the woman knew what was taking place but they were also cast out in the name of Jesus.

Back to Wesley,

> When I was come, I was quite cold and dead and fitter for sleep than prayer. She burst out into a horrid laughter and said, "No power, no power; no faith, no faith. She is mine; her soul is mine. I have her and will not let her go."

> We begged of God to increase our faith. Meanwhile her pangs increased more and more so that one would have imagined, by the violence of the throes, her body must have been shattered to pieces...We betook ourselves to prayer again and ceased not till she began, about six o'clock, with a clear voice and composed, cheerful look: (sang) Praise God, from whom all blessings flow."

We have known for many years satanists have been praying for the break up of Christian homes and marriages, especially targeting Christian leaders. Several years ago I attended a conference on evangelism organised by the Billy Graham Association. On the second evening Cliff Barrows, one of the leaders of the Billy Graham team, told the story about a friend of his who was travelling on a Greyhound bus in the United States and got talking to a young man sitting nearby. Cliff's friend offered him some food and the man told him he was a satanist and was fasting. When asked why he was doing that he replied, "I fast twice a week for Christian marriages and homes to break up and especially those of Christian leaders."

Overcoming the powers of darkness and standing against spiritual attacks is not just something than concerns us individually. We need to know how to be able to fight for our families and loved ones.

The *Gay Liberation Front Manifesto* clearly states, "We must aim at the abolition of the family, so that the sexist, male supremacist system can no longer be nurtured there...We believe that the suffocating small family unit is by no means the best atmosphere for bringing up children."

I will never forget the afternoon I had a phone call from a frantic grandparent asking to see me urgently. He had travelled with his wife and son-in-law from the south of Scotland about 160 miles and had gone to the divinity department of Aberdeen University seeking help. Hearing his story they gave him my contact details and I met him and his family in the church I pastored in the city.

He shared with me their frantic concerns for his young grandchild who was just over a year old. The house the child and her parents lived in had a history of "spiritual problems" with it turning either freezing cold or extremely hot for no obvious reasons. Foot prints mysteriously appeared on the walls and they were terrified to stay there. What was most disturbing was the behaviour of the child who started drawing hideous pictures of mutilated people. On one occasion her mother walked into the child's bedroom thinking she was asleep and found her having a grown up conversation with someone unseen. The one-year-old was using old English words and language the mother did not fully understand. When the child saw her she immediately stopped and began to speak again in baby language. The parents discovered that the site where they lived was built on an ancient battlefield where many bloody battles had been fought.

It was a harrowing story, the parents were not Christians but the grandparents were church goers and I advised them to immediately get the child out of the house and for mother and daughter to go and stay with them until better accommodation could be arranged. I told them to go and talk with their local minister and have the child baptised (they were Church of Scotland members and even though the church I belong to practices infant dedication, not christening, I felt this was not a time to debate theological issues concerning infant baptism). The child needed all the spiritual input she could receive. We prayed together and felt strongly God's peace and I encouraged them to have the child prayed for by godly people as often as they could and for they themselves to get their lives right with God through Jesus.

It is not without significance that the parts of the Bible that have been most ridiculed and attacked are the early chapters of Genesis and the latter ones of Revelation. They tell us of the devil's entry into our world, his existence, how he operates and his ultimate end and destruction. He doesn't want anyone to know that he is real and active, yet through the cross and resurrection he is defeated and there is coming a day when he will be cast into a lake of fire to be *"tormented day and night forever and ever."* He loves to remind us of our past but hates it when we remind him of his future.

One of the subjects my wife Jan and I were required to study in Bible College as part of our Old Testament course was called the *Documentary Hypothesis of the Pentateuch.* It involved studying the first five books of the Bible from liberal scholars' understanding where they state that it was written at different times and places by different people, Moses was not the sole author. It is referred to as the JEDP theory with each letter representing different origins for sections of the books.

To help study this confusing and ridiculous theory we took an old Bible and used different colour coding to represent the assumed writers. One evening years later we were ministering to a lady in our church who was obviously demonized. We had this particular colour coded Bible with us and had placed it beside the chair on which she was sitting. As we ministered to her she went into a demonic trance and started kicking wildly at the Bible which moments earlier she hadn't even noticed was there. She kicked the Bible away and when we brought it back she kicked it away again and then tried to tear it up. That night she was set free from a number of demons and on the way home from church my wife and I couldn't help note that though many liberal Bible scholars don't believe God's word, demons certainly do.

David Pawson in his book, *Unlocking the Bible* says that he has remarkable proof of Satan's particular hatred of Revelation 20. Many cassette recordings of his exposition of this chapter have been damaged between despatch and receipt. In some cases the section dealing with the devil's doom has been wiped clean before reaching its destination; in others a screaming voice using foreign language has been superimposed rendering the original words unintelligible!

When it comes to spiritual warfare God wants us to be wise and informed, *"Not ignorant of satan's schemes,"* 2 Corinthians 2:11. The Apostle Peter warns us to, *"Be self-controlled and alert. Your enemy (adversary) the devil prowls around like a roaring lion looking for someone to devour,"* 1 Peter 5:8. The devil hates Christians because we love God, but that's not the only reason. He hates because it is his character. Even those who serve him he despises because it is the nature of who he is.

In his book *Your Adversary the Devil* Dwight Pentecost compares the tactics of a physical battle to those of a spiritual one,

> "No military commander could expect to be victorious in battle unless he understood his enemy. Should he prepare for an attack by land and ignore the possibility that the enemy might

approach by air or by sea, he would open the way to defeat. Or should he prepare for a land and sea attack and ignore the possibility of an attack through the air, and he would certainly jeopardise the campaign. No individual can be victorious against the adversary of our souls unless he understands that adversary; unless he understands his philosophy, his methods of operation, his methods of temptation."

Satan chooses his strategies to correspond to the vulnerabilities of his targets whether they are individuals, groups, communities or towns and cities.

When I went to pastor in Scotland the area the church was situated in was near the harbour in the red light district. There were three churches in this vicinity and each of the ministers had been exposed as being involved in immoral practices. One was given a three year jail sentence. The second was removed from ministry. The minister in the church before me had also been removed because of sexual immorality. As soon as I arrived at the church and discovered what had been taking place I immediately knew that spiritual attack in the sexual realm was intense. I shared this with the leadership of the fellowship and we humbled ourselves before God and prayed powerfully into it. During the next 15 years I pastored the church we never had any leadership issues or problems in this area.

Everyone one of us is born into a spiritual war whether we like it or not. The question we have to answer is will we live our lives as victims or as victors?

In his booklet *Defensive Spiritual Warfare,* the late Tom Marshall provides a fascinating insight into the devil's activity and attacks in the business, political and corporate realm. He says,

A business, a corporation or a church for that matter, has an inner life that is actually spirit. We are spirit beings and when we corporately create an organisation there comes into being a corporate spirit. This thing is alive, it seeks to manage, control and even dominate people. You can go to meetings and seminars and know after a short time what company or organisation people belong to by the way they talk, act, and respond. They have a corporate and organizational identity. This corporate spirit (unless infused by the power of the Holy Spirit) is not only alive but is fallen and idolatrous and has two main aims:

It will do anything to survive.

It will do anything to succeed.

Marshall says he recalls watching a television interview with the then New Zealand Prime Minister who was asked by the interviewer what is the first principle of government. The Prime Minister did not answer to govern justly or for the benefit of the people but replied that the first principle of Government is to stay in power. In other words anything to survive. It reminded me of a political commentator I heard reporting on the White House in America, "What this administration wants above all else is what every first term administration desires, another term of office."

The second aspect of an ungodly corporation/administration spirit is that it will do whatever is necessary to succeed. The Watergate scandal in 1972 is a terrifying and tragic example of this. Richard Nixon is the only American president forced to resign the office. The tape recordings he took in his office revealed to Congress and the world that his role in the cover-up began as early as six days after the break-in. The tapes also reveal an immense scope of crimes and abuses that predate the Watergate break-in. These include campaign fraud, political espionage and sabotage, illegal break-ins, improper tax audits, illegal wiretapping on a massive scale and a secret slush fund laundered in Mexico to pay those who conducted these operations. Significantly, more that 30 years before while a law student at Duke University, the young Richard Nixon, along with two friends broke into the Dean's office to learn what their academic standing was which would affect their future prospects.

Writing in the updated preface to his book *The Screwtape Letters* C S Lewis said,

> "I live in the Managerial Age, in a world of 'Admin.' The greatest evil is not now done in those sordid 'dens of crime' that Dickens loved to paint. It is not even done in concentration camps and labour camps. In those we see its final result. But it is conceived and ordered (moved, seconded, carried and minuted) in clean, carpeted, warmed, and well-lighted offices, by quiet men with white collars and cut fingernails and smooth shaven cheeks who do not need to raise their voice. Hence, naturally enough, my symbol for hell is something like the bureaucracy of a police state or the offices of a thoroughly nasty business concern."

It is no longer church spires that dominate the skylines of towns and cities. It is the banks, financial institutions and multinational companies. Their prominence is not only a commercial and social statement of importance but also a spiritual one. The modern day cathedrals are now the huge shopping centres and sports stadia, with the major sporting finals and events taking place on a Sunday.

The British East India Company which dominated trade in the East during the time of the British Empire did everything it could to oppose Christian missionary work in India. They did not want the indigenous population educated and able to run their own national interests as that would inhibit their own business trading. They were particularly hostile to the great missionary William Carey when he arrived there in the 18th century and would not allow him to establish a mission base in their jurisdiction.

Joel Bakan's critically acclaimed best selling book and film *The Corporation: The Pathological Pursuit of Profit and Power*, is both fascinating and frightening. The book and documentary show the development of the contemporary business corporation, from a legal entity that originated as a government-chartered institution meant to effect specific public functions, to the rise of the modern commercial institution entitled to most of the legal rights of a person. Robert Hare, a University of British Columbia psychology professor and a consultant to the FBI, frighteningly compares the profile of the contemporary business corporation to that of a clinically-diagnosed psychopath. The book and the film state the principle enshrined in law that the managers and directors of a company have a legal duty to put shareholders' interests above all others – what matters most is the bottom line. It is what has become known as "the best interests of the corporation principle." Such drive for profit has created the "sweat shops" of the Third World producing garments for which workers are paid a few pence and which the companies charge a hundred times more for on the high street. It is also why, as shown in the film, big business is willing to work with any regime so long as profits are to be made. It presents the startling fact that in one week alone 57 US companies were fined for trading with enemies of the country.

The pursuit of profit is also highlighted by the actions of two of the world's biggest corporations. We are told how a punch card system devised and regularly maintained by IBM (operating out of New York) processed millions of concentration camp victims during World War II. Only after Jews were identified – a massive and complex task that Hitler wanted done immediately – could they be targeted for efficient asset confiscation, ghettoisation, deportation, enslaved labour, and ultimately, annihilation. It was a cross-tabulation and organizational challenge so monumental, it called for a computer. Of course, in the 1930s no such computers existed, but IBM's Hollerith punch card technology did exist, aided by the company's custom-designed and constantly updated Hollerith systems. While IBM admits such use of its products and expertise it denies active collaboration with Nazi Germany, however, Edwin Blacks, in his book *IBM and the Holocaust* documents the company's involvement.

Bakan also points to Coca-Cola for its business activities in Nazi Germany. While Coke was storming through Europe in the 1940s supporting American GIs, Coca-Cola (Germany) advertised its products in the Nazi press and built bottling plants in occupied territories. Then in 1941, when Coca-Cola Germany could no longer get the syrup from America to make Coke, it invented a new drink specifically for the Nazi beverage market out of the ingredients available to it. That drink was Fanta.

We read in Isaiah 47:8 that the spirit at work in Babylon proudly declares, *"I am, and there is none beside me. I will never be a widow or suffer the loss of children."* Revelation 17-18 tells us this spirit of Babylon operates and controls the world's markets and financial systems. The great declaration of Revelation 19:6 *"Hallelujah! For our Lord God Almighty reigns,"* is in response to the collapse of these world financial markets.

This demonic spirit manifests itself when it has an idolatrous drive that wants to dominate people and to be the ultimate authority in their lives. It seeks to shape their values and ethical standards. Christians working in such environments need to be aware of what is going on around them and be indwelt by the power of the Holy Spirit to keep them free from the domination of business power. Like Daniel in Babylon and Joseph in Egypt we can work within the most hostile surroundings and maintain our integrity and serve God because we have righteous and legitimate ends.

Lovers of chocolate have a lot to thank George Cadbury for, but he was far more than a very successful businessman. First and foremost he was a Christian and this affected everything he did. Despite the demands of running a large company, he was committed to spending time helping those less privileged than himself. Cadbury often said, "We can do nothing of any value to God, except in acts of genuine helpfulness done to our fellow men."

Cadbury built hundreds of new "superior" houses for his workers and established schools. His was among the first companies to introduce paid holidays and shorter working weeks, he provided medical and dental treatment for all his employees and their families and paid £60,000 (a huge amount at the time) into a pension fund for his workers. In the grounds of his home, Northfield Manor, Cadbury arranged for the construction of a building that could seat 700 people. Every year during the summer months, Cadbury provided food and entertainment for about 25,000 children from the deprived areas of Birmingham.

He once said,

> "I have for many years given practically the whole of my income for charitable purposes, except what is spent upon my family. Nearly all

> my money is invested in businesses in which I believe I can truly say the first thought is for the welfare of the people employed."

Robert LeTourneau was an American businessman and prolific inventor who was perhaps one of the most influential individuals in the earthmoving industry. He had close to 300 patents credited to his name for such inventions as bulldozers, scrapers, dredgers, portable cranes, rollers, dump wagons, bridge spans, logging equipment, mobile sea platforms for oil exploration, and the electric wheel, just to name a few. More than anything else he was a follower of Jesus and his colleagues called him "God's businessman." Throughout his life, he combined a passion for the earthmoving business with a passion for evangelism. As his company grew, he and his wife became famous for giving 90 per cent of their personal and corporate income to charitable Christian causes, primarily through his own foundation that supported religious, missionary and educational endeavours. He also incorporated his religious beliefs in the workplace by hiring three full-time chaplains in his manufacturing plants.

This is what can happen when a godly spirit is at work within a company and its bosses.

Satan believes we all have a price and probes for our weaknesses – he thinks that every person has a place of battlefield vulnerability. He strives to discover what that is and will do anything to find it. He believes that every one of us can be bought and have a breaking point and that is what he is after.

In the next chapter we are going to see a man who came under intense spiritual attack, financially, socially, mentally and physically and yet was able to stand and succeed.

2

Why Do Bad Things Happen To Good People?

God, who foresaw your tribulation, has specially
armed you to go through it, not without
pain but without stain
C S Lewis

As a young minister pastoring my first church I vividly remember visiting an elderly lady dying with cancer. She was a long standing member of the church and a wonderful godly woman. On one occasion I entered her home to hear her screaming in pain. The stomach cancer and its effects were at times unbearable. When she saw me she said, "Pastor, make the pain go, please make it go." I believe in God's miraculous intervention and have seen it many times but at that moment I felt out of my depth and overwhelmed by her cries for help. I quickly prayed and almost immediately the doctor knocked the front door and arrived with morphine which quickly took away her anguish. A few months later I took part in her funeral service which was a victorious event. She had loved and served God and was now free from all suffering and gone home to her heavenly reward. Yet the questions remain for us as to why do good people suffer? Why do bad things happen to them? Why is there so much suffering and pain in our world?

Bad things do happen to good people and the confusion and pain they cause is one of the heaviest loads we have to bear. Life isn't always fair. We live in a "fallen world" surrounded by fallen and broken people with all the problems and suffering this brings.

It's significant that the book of Job which addresses the issue of suffering is, according to most scholars, the oldest book in the Bible. Many phrases we use in the English language come straight from the book. We speak of "Job's comforters" and "the patience of Job" but generally the book is not very well known apart from the first few chapters and the last one.

One of the first questions we must ask about Job is whether or not he was a real person and if the book is fact or fiction. Did these events actually take place the way they are described or is it simply some kind of ancient Aesop's fable teaching moral and spiritual truths?

There is no doubt that other Biblical writers regard Job as a real person and Ezekiel lists him with Noah and Daniel as one of the three most righteous people who ever lived, (Ezekiel 14:4). James 5 encourages us to be patient like Job in the midst of suffering. But there are some difficulties in regarding the book of Job as an absolute factual account. To start with the story seems far too neatly arranged. In chapter one we read four times after each tragedy, four different messengers announcing to Job the exact same phrase, *"and I am the only one who has escaped to tell you!"* Job 1:15,16,17,19.

Not only that but each speech in Job, and there are lots of them, is written in Hebrew poetry. Such expressions are an artificial form of conversational speaking, yet all Job's friends speak in superbly crafted poems. People do not normally talk that way. In fact we do the exact opposite to try and help those who are hurting. Poetic language has its place but not usually with those whose lives are falling apart with grief.

Are we then saying the book of Job is not factual? Not at all. The book is based on actual events that took place. Job and his family are real but under the Holy Spirit's anointing the events have been presented in a dramatic and even dramatized way into a superbly crafted story. So in the oldest book of scripture we are given an insight into the age old question God knew would be asked more than any other concerning Him and this world, "If God is so good and so great why do bad things happen to good people?" It's the heartbreak of a mother and father whose child has died of an incurable ailment. It's the anguish of seeing a loved one suffer and die who should have had many more years to live. I recently received an e-mail telling of a storm in northern India that destroyed a brand new Christian school and church, killing a five-year-old child. I read about a Christian mother who was killed when a fuel tanker ploughed into the back of her car, she was on her way to a mission's conference. How do you try and come to terms with such things and a "zillion" others in our world with 24 hour news giving us graphic images of the latest innocent victims of a terrorist bomb, natural disaster or a mad man's killing spree?

I have a good friend who in the course of several years went from being a highly successful minister, to being betrayed by fellow church leaders, suffering a breakdown, clinical depression and subsequent cancer. He saw his family suffer and sadly his marriage fail due to all the pain and pressures. He is a good and godly man who made huge sacrifices in following God. I asked him how he managed to cope and maintain his spiritual passion. He said jokingly, yet seriously, "I read the book of Job and trust in God." Miraculously God healed him from the cancer and he is now ministering again.

Martin Luther, the Protestant reformer, was no stranger to suffering in his life. We may sing his great hymn, *A Mighty Fortress is our God,* and suppose he never questioned his faith, but he once wrote, "For more than a week, Christ was wholly lost. I was shaken by desperation and blasphemy against God." His wife Katarina had a miscarriage, his beloved 13-year-old daughter Magdelena died of a sudden illness and his own health failed yet through it all he was sustained by God's grace. It is not surprising therefore that he said the book of Job is magnificent and sublime as no other book in scripture.

Parallel Dimensions
Understanding the Spiritual Realm

> *One day the angels came to present themselves before the Lord, and Satan also came with them. The Lord said to Satan, "Where have you come from?" Satan answered the Lord, "From roaming through the earth and going back and forth in it." Then the Lord said to Satan, "Have you considered my servant Job? There is no one on earth like him; he is blameless and upright, a man who fears God and shuns evil."*
>
> Job 1:6-8

The book of Job opens with an account of a man and his family on earth and a scene in heaven where the devil comes before God. Whereas God says how righteous Job is the devil immediately slanders and accuses him. So the pattern is set, God is our defender and Satan our accuser. In the last book of the Bible we see this continuing with the devil being the *"accuser of the brethren"* (Revelation 12:10) and Jesus being our defender and deliverer.

It also shows us that the devil and his demons are not in hell, the devil dwells in spiritual and moral darkness wherever it is found. In Job 1 Satan is shown walking to and fro in the earth and Peter tells us to, *"Be self-controlled and alert. Your enemy the devil prowls around like a roaring lion looking for someone to devour,"* 1 Peter 5:8. Paul, in the book of Ephesians explains that the devil and the demonic powers we wrestle against are in the heavenly realms, Ephesians 6:10. Five times in this epistle Paul mentions *"The heavenly realms"* which is the spiritual dimension that is all around us – a parallel realm of reality.

We live in a physical world inhabited by flesh and blood but around us, just as real, there is a spiritual domain inhabited by angelic and demonic powers. It's reckoned even in our physical world only about 10 per cent is visible to us. There are atoms and particles, radio waves and frequencies. Get a microscope and you can see them or a radio and you can tune in. It's the same with the spiritual dimension, all you need are the right spiritual senses to comprehend it. But some are like the young child who complained because he was told to wash his hands before dinner, "Jesus and germs, Jesus and germs, that's all my parents tell me and I haven't seen either of them!"

To try and understand why there is such suffering in this world and why bad things happen to good people the book of Job introduces us straight away to these two parallel dimensions – there is heaven and earth, a physical realm we inhabit and the spiritual realm inhabited by spiritual powers and forces coexisting with each other.

This spiritual realm constantly seeks to be involved in the physical world and our physical world continually tries to contact and communicate with the spiritual dimension. If you encounter the spiritual realm and do not have the protection of Jesus Christ you open your life to deception and destruction.

Take for instance one of the most famous rock songs ever written, Led Zeppelin's *Stairway to Heaven*. It is a rock classic which is in reality a stairway to hell. Robert Plant belts out the lyrics,

> *"If there's a bustle in your hedgerow*
> *Don't be alarmed now.*
> *It's just a spring clean for the May Queen.*
> *Yes there are two paths you can go by.*
> *But in the long run*
> *There's still time to change the road you are on."*

The real message, however, is heard when that part of the song is played backwards using a technique call "Backward Masking," which has attracted a great deal of interest and controversy, then the lyrics are,

> *"I sing because I live with Satan.*
> *The Lord turns me off.*
> *There's no escaping it.*
> *No other made path.*
> *Here's to my sweet Satan.*
> *Who's power is Satan*
> *He will give you 666.*
> *I live for Satan."*

Zeppelin's lead guitarist, Jimmy Page, owned an occult bookstore in Kensington, London. He also owned and lived in a castle that was once the home of one of the most evil men of the 19th century – Aleister Crowley – the self proclaimed "Beast 666."

Who really wrote this song? Listen to what Robert Plant had to say about how the lyrics came about,

> "I was just sitting with Page in front of a fire at
> Headley Grange. Pagey had written the chords

and played them for me. I was holding a piece of paper and pencil and for some reason I was in a very bad mood. Then all of a sudden my hand was writing out the words, 'There's a lady who's sure, that all that glitters is gold, and she's buying a stairway to heaven.' I just sat there and looked at the words and then almost leaped out of my seat."

In his book *Mein Kampf*, Adolf Hitler wrote, "If Germany does not conquer then it will bring the whole to destruction with it." Nazism was founded on occultic and demonic philosophical beliefs and practices. Hitler and many of his closest aides were obsessed with them. Their hatred of the Jews and the holocaust that murdered millions was driven by dark demonic forces.

In his definitive work on Nazi Germany *The Rise and Fall of The Third Reich,* W L Shirer records the influence of Houston Stuart Chamberlain, whose writings and ideas fuelled the beliefs of Hitler and National Socialism. Chamberlain was one of the first intellectuals in Germany to see a "great" political and military future for Hitler and the nation. He met Hitler for the first time in 1923 in Bayreuth (and visited him several times after that), he was so impressed that he wrote to him the next day, "You have mighty things to do." During 1923 and 1926, he also met frequently with Joseph Goebbels.

Shirer describes Chamberlain as,

"Hypersensitive and neurotic and subject to frequent nervous breakdowns. A man given to seeing demons who, by his own account, drove him relentlessly to seek new fields of study. One vision after another forced him to change from biology to botany to the fine arts to music to

33

> philosophy to biography to history. Once, in 1896
> when he was returning from Italy, the presence of
> a demon became so forceful that he got off the
> train at Gardone, shut himself up in a hotel room
> for eight days and abandoning work on music that
> he had contemplated, wrote feverishly on a
> biological thesis until he had the germ of the
> theme that would dominate all his later works –
> *Race and History.*"

In his book *Foundations of the Nineteenth Century* Chamberlain
provided the Nazis with many of their racial beliefs and aberrations
on the supremacy of their race and purity of their bloodline. This
1200 page book Chamberlain said he wrote while possessed by a
demon. He claimed it was the key to history, civilization and race.
More than a quarter of a million copies sold in Germany by 1938.

God's kingdom also desires to enter into our physical world. One
of the greatest books ever written was by Harriet Beecher Stowe,
called *Uncle Tom's Cabin.* It exposed across America and beyond
the cruelty and evil of slavery. It sold 300,000 copies in America in
its first year and was a phenomenon, (in one year in Great Britain it
sold one and a half million copies). This book more than any other
work of literature except the Bible helped to pull down the
stronghold of slavery in America. How it came to be written is
quite fascinating. Harriet Beecher's father was the Rev Lyman
Beecher, a distinguished man, who in the early 1800s spoke out
strongly against slavery and the slave trade. Harriet Beecher's son
reveals how the conception of Uncle Tom and the story came
about,

> "It was in the month of February (1851) that Mrs
> Stowe was seated at the communion service in the
> college church at Brunswick. Suddenly, like the

unrolling of a picture, the scene of the death of Uncle Tom passed before her mind. So strongly was she affected that it was with difficulty she could keep from weeping aloud. Immediately on returning home she took pen and paper and wrote out the vision which had been, as it were, blown into her mind as by the rushing of a mighty wind."

When C S Lewis started writing *The Lion, The Witch and The Wardrobe* he says there wasn't anything Christian about the story. He said he simply wanted to write a fairy tale for children and didn't have a storyline planned out until Aslan (a lion representing Jesus) came leaping into the book. He was pretty far into the story before he even thought of Aslan. He tells how he had been dreaming of lions in his sleep and realised that this was the story's missing element. He describes Aslan as, "Bounding into the story and everything then fell into place."

On the other side of the fence so to speak, J K Rowling describes how she came to write about Harry Potter which has made witchcraft "fun" and fascinating to millions of children.

Rowling says she came up with the idea for her books in 1990. While travelling on a train and without any warning she suddenly just saw Harry "very, very clearly." Into her mind his visible image suddenly came and from out of "nowhere" a fully formed individual. During one interview she gave she said, "The character of Harry just strolled into my head...I really did feel he was someone who walked up and introduced himself in my mind's eye." She confesses that she has no idea why he chose to "come to her" when he did. According to her account Harry just stood there looking very much like he does now on the cover of her books, complete with black hair and spectacles. She somehow perceived that he was a wizard and knew that he did not know he was a wizard. Soon afterward, she began thinking about how this could possibly be, and before long, was writing about a young boy who did not know he had magical powers – Harry Potter was born.

Samuel Morse, the inventor of the Morse Code, was once asked if he ever encountered situations where he didn't know what to do. Morse responded, "More than once, and whenever I could not see my way clearly, I knelt down and prayed to God for light and understanding." Morse sent the first message by his code from Baltimore to Washington, it consisted of just four words, "What God hath wrought." He wrote to his brother that this was God's work and "He alone could have carried me thus far through all my trials." Morse received many honours from his invention of the telegraph but felt undeserving, "I have made a valuable application of electricity not because I was superior to other men but solely because God, who meant it for mankind, must reveal it to someone and He was pleased to reveal it to me," he said.

James Simpson was a brilliant scientist who more than anyone else pioneered the use of chloroform. While a student at Edinburgh University in the 19th century he was attracted to surgery because he was troubled by the pain and mortality rate experienced during operations. As a result of reading Genesis 2:21, *"So the Lord God caused a deep sleep to fall upon Adam..."* Simpson thought that chloroform might be the answer and by it alleviated the suffering of millions. Other surgeons would not use it at first, many were suspicious and jealous and it was only when Queen Victoria used it for pain relief for the delivery of her eighth child, Prince Leopold, that it became widely accepted. When Simpson was asked years later, "What do you regard as your greatest discovery?" He replied, "My greatest discovery was Jesus Christ as my Saviour." He wrote, "In Christ you will find a companion, a friend, a brother who loves you with a greater love than a human heart can conceive."

Back to Job

The book of Job reveals to us that we will never be able to have any understanding of suffering in our world unless we realise there is another realm beside the physical and also that there is another life after this one. In the depths of his suffering Job makes some of the greatest faith and worship statements in the whole Bible. These are not the product of a philosophical belief – pain and tragedy expose how hollow such things as mere religion and philosophy are. They have no life in the face of heartache and death. But when Job hears the heartbreaking news about his children we are told,

> *At this, Job got up and tore his robe and shaved his head. Then he fell to the ground in worship and said: "Naked I came from my mother's womb, and naked I will depart. The Lord gave and the Lord has taken away; may the name of the Lord be praises."*
>
> Job 1:20,21

Later, when Job is afflicted with sickness and his flesh becomes a mass of boils and sores, he declares,

> *I know that my Redeemer lives, and that in the end he will stand upon the earth. And after my skin has been destroyed, yet in my flesh I will see God; I myself will see him with my own eyes – I, and not another. How my heart yearns within me!*
>
> Job 19:25-27

This is the first reference to redemption and the resurrection in the Bible. It's the faith of a man who says, "I don't know why all this has happened to me or why it's been allowed to happen, but I do know this, I have a Redeemer and even if my body is destroyed

37

and life taken from me, that is not the end of the story for I will see God and a greater life is to come." Later he says, *"When I have been refined I shall come forth like gold,"* Job 23:10. He recognises there is a purpose to what is happening. Job's trust in God enabled him to stand and declare God's love and power against every attack he faced.

In one of his books depicting the adventures of a British soldier called Sharpe (made into a successful television series) Bernard Cornwell has him making an impassioned and powerful speech on the eve of battle at a place called Talavera in Spain. Sharpe is fighting with Wellington against Napoleon and preparing his company *The South Essex* for the conflict ahead. Many of them had never experienced battle before and Sharpe says,

> "Tomorrow, over that ridge there will come a column of French infantry, not a pretty sight, they are brave men marching not in line but in column. You don't see a battle when it starts, but you do hear it and smell it – the noise of the drum, the chant of the enemy, the explosion of gun powder and the relentless advance of marching men. You shoot them but they keep coming. If you panic you run and turn your backs and then they will charge and break through your lines, and Napoleon has won another battle. But if you can stand in the midst of it all and fire three rounds a minute and keep standing and keep firing then they will eventually stop and retreat and we will break through their lines. I know you can fire three rounds a minute, you have been trained, you have practiced, but what I want to know is can you do it and keep doing it in battle, amidst the

screams, the smoke, the conflict and the confusion? I know you can shoot but can you stand?"

It was a remarkable speech and the British won an historic victory, not just because the soldiers were good shots but they were able to stand and fire when under attack. This is what distinguishes us not only in physical warfare but also in spiritual conflict. We may know our Bibles, sing all the latest worship songs, been to all the spiritual warfare conferences and we can fire three shots a minute (or quote more than three scriptures a minute) but can we stand in the midst of trial and adversity when the enemy is coming over the hill and keep firing, keep believing and praising God?

In 60 years of active ministry William Booth the founder of the Salvation Army preached over 60,000 sermons and deployed two million "soldiers" in 55 nations. He was the first Christian leader to be received as such by the Japanese Emperor. With little formal education an honorary degree was conferred on him by Oxford University.

But such recognition did not come easily. He was criticized by the rich and abused by the poor. When his early soldiers began preaching in front of saloons and pubs mobs of ruffians and drunks were instigated to disrupt and stop if possible his efforts. He and his workers often returned to their quarters with bloodied faces and rotten egg spattered uniforms. One press headline said they were pelted with live coals and even dead cats. The women wore black straw bonnets specially designed with a tilted rim to deflect flying missiles.

But they kept on preaching and marching for Jesus. The reason for their amazing success was not only could they shoot "three rounds a minute" but they were able to stand in the midst of spiritual and sometimes physical battle and keep on firing.

When he was invited to be presented to King Edward VII Booth was granted the unusual privilege of being allowed to wear his Salvation Army uniform and cape instead of the usually required formal frock and coat, and equally unusual was the monarch's shaking him by the hand (almost never done) as he said, "You are doing a good work, a great work."

Booth's funeral in 1912 was such that his lying in state had to be extended to three days while 150,000 people filed past. Then came the funeral in the huge London exhibition hall where some 40,000 people crowded in. It is reckoned that unknown to most royalty was there too as Queen Mary, who was a stanch admirer of William Booth, decided to attend at the last moment without warning.

Thank God for such a man. His very last speech summed up his life. "While women weep, as they do now, I'll fight, while little children go hungry, I'll fight; while men go to prison, in and out, in and out, as they do now, I'll fight; while there is a drunkard left, while there is a poor lost girl upon the streets, where there remains one dark soul without the light of God I'll fight! I'll fight to the very end."

When Martin Luther was summoned to renounce his beliefs at the Diet (council) of Worms on 17 April, 1521, he requested time to think about his answer. Granted an extension, Luther prayed, consulted with friends and mediators and presented himself before the Diet the following day. When the counsellor put the same question to Luther he respectfully but boldly stated,

> "Unless I am convinced by proofs from scriptures
> or by plain and clear reasons and arguments, I can
> and will not retract, for it is neither safe nor wise
> to do anything against conscience. Here I stand. I
> can do no other. God help me. Amen."

Job did finally ask God why such things had happened to him. But God doesn't reveal it to him, perhaps because Job wouldn't understand. He simply reveals more of Himself and asks Job over seventy questions. He shows Job how little he knew and how great God's ways and works are.

But that's not the end of the story. Job is healed, his comforters are rebuked and his fortunes restored and increased. He is also blessed with seven more sons and three daughters. Often the significance of this as far as Job's children are concerned is overlooked. Job received 14,000 sheep to replace 7,000; 6,000 camels to replaces 3,000; 1,000 donkeys to replace 500. There is one exception, previously he had seven sons and three daughters, and in the restoration he had seven more sons and three daughters – the same number – not double. But from an eternal perspective Job did receive double, ten new children in this life along with the ten children in the life to come.

Marshall Shelley is the editor of a major Christian leadership journal in America. He and his wife have five children, four girls and one boy, of whom three are living on this earth, two are living in heaven. His daughter Mandy died just two weeks short of her second birthday and three months earlier his son Toby was born but lived just a few minutes. Shelley and his wife struggled in their grief with the question, why would God create a child to live for just two years or even two minutes? They came to the understanding that God had not created their daughter to live for two years. Neither had He created their son to live for just two minutes. God had created them for eternity. They still had a family of five children.

After serving as a missionary for forty years in Africa, Henry C. Morrison became sick and had to return to America. As the great ocean liner docked in New York Harbour there was a great crowd gathered to welcome home another passenger on that boat. Morrison watched as President Teddy Roosevelt received a grand welcome home party after his African safari.

Resentment seized Henry Morrsion and he complained to God, "I have come back home after all this time and service to the church and there is no one, not even one person here to welcome me home."

Then, in a still small voice Morrison said God spoke to him, "Remember, you're not home yet."

We can only begin to answer the question why does God allow suffering and bad things to happen to good people when we realise there is another dimension besides the one we see with our physical senses and there is another life after this one is over.

Our world is not how He made it. Man's sin and rebellion have come at a great cost. There will come a day when God will finally stop all the suffering but the reason He has not done so yet is that *"He is patient not wanting anyone to perish, but everyone to come to repentance,"* 2 Peter 3:9.

When Jesus came He did not try to explain away suffering, He did something far more amazing, He took it upon Himself. For the worst thing that ever happened to a good person took place when He was nailed to a cross.

3

Disappointed With God

Though our feelings come and go,
God's love for us does not.
C S Lewis

In his book *Disappointed with God,* Philip Yancey tells of a time in his life when he was struggling to find certainty of faith. One day, as he was randomly surfing the television channels, he came across a mass healing service being conducted by Kathryn Kuhlman. He was intrigue and delighted by the miracles he saw and testimonies of healings he heard. A few weeks later he attended one of the services and was especially struck by the testimony of a man from Milwaukee who had been carried into the meeting on a stretcher. He told the congregation he was a doctor who had incurable lung cancer and was given just six months to live. But that night he testified he believed God had healed him and he was walking for the first time in months. Yancey says he was elated and wrote down the man's name and says he practically floated out of that meeting. One week later he phoned Directory Assistance in Milwaukee and got the doctor's telephone number.

"When I dialed it, a woman answered the phone. 'May I please speak to Dr S_____,' I said. Long silence. 'Who are you?' she said at last. I figured she was just screening calls from patients or something. I gave my name and told her I admired Dr S_____ and had wanted to talk to him ever since the Kathryn Kuhlman meeting. I had been very moved by his story, I said. Another long silence. Then she spoke in a flat voice, pronouncing each word slowly.

"'My...husband...is...dead.' Just that one sentence, nothing more, and she hung up. I can't tell you how that devastated me. I was wasted...A flame had flared bright for one fine, shining week and then gone dark, like a dying star."

Philip Yancey has become a best selling Christian writer and the ministry of Kathryn Kuhlman saw thousands of verified healings and miracles that stood the test of time. But what Yancey describes does honestly reflect the highs and lows Christians experience with their faith.

There are times when we are simply delighted with God and life could not be better. Then there are those days when we are confused, discouraged and disappointed. The prayer was not answered the way we expected. The provision we asked God for has not come. A loved one we are praying for is getting worse and we wonder where is God? During such times we tend to let down our shields of faith and every fiery dart of the devil hits its target. We become vulnerable, fragile, confused and the strength and fight have been knocked out of us.

The prophet Elijah knew what this was like. After his famous victory on Mount Carmel against the false prophets in Israel he becomes afraid at Jezebel's threats and runs away into the desert wanting to die. Hours before he had been so strong and now he felt so weak. Elijah had expected the nation to turn to God but it wasn't happening. Instead Jezebel with all her demonic fury unleashes her venom against him. This was not the first time she had tried to have him killed but it was the first time she had caused him to fear and run scared. Thank God the story doesn't end there, Elijah is restored and Jezebel is destroyed but it does show that when our expectations of God fail so can we.

The late Selwyn Hughes, who wrote the popular daily devotional *Every Day with Jesus*, was once asked in a radio interview, "Over the many years in which you have been a minister and counsellor, what has been the biggest single problem you have come across in the lives of fellow Christians? Unhesitatingly he replied, "Disappointment with God, because of something He did not do or something He did not provide." And when further asked what he thought the reason was for this he explained it was because of a misunderstanding of who God is.

He went on to explain, "Many Christians go through life with suppressed disappointment and anger because at some point in their experience God did not come through for them the way they thought He should. They prayed for God to heal but it didn't happen. They prayed for God's provision but life got harder. They asked God to save loved ones but they are still unsaved. Time, it says, is a great healer and many Christians recover from negative feelings about God but often there is no real healing, just covering the emotions and living with confusion. When some crisis hits and God does not come up to expectations the submerged feelings break out and the problems begin all over again. The sooner we learn to accept God as He is and not imagine Him as we would like

Him the sooner we will move from the path of confusion to confidence."

What Hughes highlights is one of the major reasons Christians become vulnerable to spiritual attacks. It's why many believers start the spiritual race well but finish badly. They may have come to salvation after a powerful encounter with God through healing or deliverance. But then there came a time when God didn't heal and provision and prayer was not answered as they expected and doubt, disappointment and confusion sets in.

Hughes also suggests the reason so many Christians become disappointed with God is because they do not have what can best be described as a bottom line (foundation truth understanding) of who God is. So when they cannot make sense of a situation this foundational truth upholds them and explains Him.

What is your "foundational understanding" of God? Is it that God is a healer? He is, but that cannot be our bottom line for there are times when those prayed for are not healed. Is it that God is a deliverer? He is, but what about those who experience persecution and are martyred for their faith? Last year there were over 300,000 Christian martyrs in our world. Is it that God is a provider? He is but at times He moves in mysterious ways and we don't always know what's best for us and the provision we expect doesn't take place.

We are introduced in the very first chapter of the Bible to the absolute "bottom line" truth of who God is. Genesis 1 tells us that He is not only a great God, but He is a good God, everything He does is *"good."* This means He is absolutely righteous, perfect and just in all He is and does.

When the serpent tempted Eve in Genesis 3, it didn't question God's existence or power but rather His goodness. So the stage was set for millennia to come. The major battle has not been over God's greatness but His goodness.

When Moses wanted to know more of God, he says to Him,

> *"Now show me your glory." And the Lord said, "I will cause all my **goodness** to pass in front of you, and I will proclaim my name, the Lord, in your presence. I will have mercy on whom I will have mercy, and I will have compassion on whom I will have compassion."*
>
> Exodus 33:18-20

One of the great themes of praise and worship in the Old Testament was, *"Give thanks to the Lord for He is good and His love endures forever,"* 1 Chronicles 16:34. The psalmist proclaims, *"O taste and see that God is good."* David reflecting on God's protection and provision, whether in green pastures or through dark valleys, says, *"Surely goodness and mercy will follow me all the days of my life and I will dwell in the house of the Lord forever."* In the New Testament Paul declares that even though not all things may be good, nevertheless when we live for God *"He makes all things work together for good,"* Romans 8:28.

Paul's life was filled with signs and wonders but also scars and wounds. He knew miraculous provision and protection and also times when he was brutalised and persecuted. He was thrown in prison many times and we love the story of his time in Philippi when he and Silas were singing hymns of praise at midnight, God sent an earthquake and the jailer and his family were saved. Many years later Paul was in prison for the final time awaiting trial but now there would be no earth shaking, only the footsteps of a Roman executioner. Paul's last letters to Timothy, describe the time,

I know whom I have believed, and am convinced that he is able to guard what I have entrusted to him for that day.

1 Timothy 1:12

For I am already being poured out like a drink offering, and the time has come for my departure. I have fought the good fight, I have finished the race, I have kept the faith.

2 Timothy 2:6-7

Paul is saying it doesn't matter whether God sends an earthquake or the devil sends an executioner, he is convinced of God's love and goodness whatever happens.

It was this understanding of God's goodness that enabled Corrie ten Boom and her sister Betsie to endure the anguish of a German concentration camp. She says, "Often I have heard people say, 'How good God is! We prayed that it would not rain for our church picnic, and look at the lovely weather!' Yes, God is good when He sends good weather. But God was also good when He allowed my sister, Betsie, to starve to death before my eyes in a German concentration camp. I remember one occasion when I was very discouraged there. Everything around us was dark, and there was darkness in my heart. I remember telling Betsie that I thought God had forgotten us. 'No, Corrie,' said Betsie, 'He has not forgotten us. Remember His Word, *"For as the heavens are high above the earth, so great is His steadfast love toward those who fear Him."'* Corrie concludes, "There is an ocean of God's love available – there is plenty for everyone. May God grant you never to doubt that victorious love – whatever the circumstances."

George Mueller was a leader in the Plymouth Brethren and the founder and director of orphanages in England during the

48

nineteenth century. He was known for his faith and prayer life. He experienced a severe test of his faith when on February 6, 1870, his beloved wife, Mary, died of rheumatic fever. She had not been well for three years and the fever overcame her in her weakened state and after six days of suffering she died.

Mueller wrote in his diary that day, "Thirty nine years and four months ago, the Lord gave me my most valuable, lovely and holy wife. Her value to me and the blessing God made her to me is beyond description. This blessing was continued to me till this day, when this afternoon about four o'clock the Lord took her to Himself."

Five days later on February 11 he wrote, "Today the earthly remains of my precious wife were laid in the grave. Many thousands of persons showed the deepest sympathy. About 1400 of the orphans who were able to walk followed in the procession...I myself, sustained by the Lord to the utmost, performed the service at the chapel and in the cemetery."

He chose Psalm 119:68 as the text of his funeral sermon *"You are good and do good."* His message had three points,

The Lord was good and did good in giving her to me.
The Lord was good and did good in so long leaving her to me.
The Lord was good and did good in taking her from me.

In discussing his third point he told how he had prayed for her during the illness, "Yes my Father, the times of my darling wife are in Thy hands. Thou wilt do the very best thing for her and me whether life or death."

A close friend reported that after the funeral Mueller sat at the vestry table, buried his face in his hands and did not speak or move for two hours. But in his loneliness and grief he could still say to the Lord, "You are good and you do good."

In his autobiography, Selwyn Hughes shares his own experiences of grief,

> "People ask how did I cope with the loss of my only two sons within ten months of each other, (one through a drink problem the other with a sudden heart attack. Years earlier his beloved wife had died of cancer). I would be less than honest if I said it did not hurt. Sometimes the pain in my soul brought hot tears to my eyes and there were times I was unable to pray. I have a little plaque in my home someone gave me years ago with just one word inscribed on it 'Jesus'. During those times when I was in so much pain that I couldn't pray, I would look at that plaque and quietly say the word 'Jesus'. In such moments God would come incredibly close to me easing the hurt in my soul. When words fail us there is one word that never fails —Jesus."

When you stand in God's love and goodness you can stand against any attack of the enemy and whatever life throws at you and there is nothing that will be able to defeat you.

4

Take the High Ground

I look to a day when people will not be judged by the colour of their skin, but by the content of their character

Martin Luther King, Jr.

At the outbreak of World War II Winston Churchill gave an impassioned speech to the House of Commons,

> "We are fighting to save the whole world from the pestilence of Nazi tyranny and in defence of all that is most sacred to man. This is no war of domination or imperial aggrandizement or material gain; no war to shut any country out of its sunlight and means of progress. It is a war, viewed in its inherent quality, to establish, on impregnable rocks, the rights of the individual, and it is a war to establish and revive the stature of man."

Several months later Churchill gave his first speech as Prime Minister. It took place after the German war machine had conquered most of mainland Europe,

> "We have before us an ordeal of the most grievous kind. We have before us many, many

51

long months of struggle and of suffering. You ask,
what is our policy? I can say: It is to wage war, by
sea, land and air, with all our might and with all
the strength that God can give us; to wage war
against a monstrous tyranny, never surpassed in
the dark, lamentable catalogue of human crime."

Churchill clearly saw the conflict with Nazi Germany as not only
fighting a great war but also a great evil. He rightly took the moral,
social and even spiritual high ground and helped the British people
to do the same. This was incredibly powerful and important during
the difficult and dark times that were ahead, such as the Blitz and
the Atlantic Siege, when the British nation was all that stood
against Nazi Germany.

In battle the high ground is the place of supreme advantage. It is
where we can more see clearly the enemy's maneouvers and from
where we can form our strategies and marshal our forces.
Battlefields can be bloody, brutal places and also very confusing
with lots of noise, smoke and fighting. The devil will try and drag
us into the confusion and the commotion. He will do all he can to
get us to focus on the confusion so we lose our peace and give in to
fear and doubt. But on the high place we can see clearly that God
is in control and we are secure in Him.

The High Place

The High Place is our position in Christ and relationship with God.
King David was a man of war, but he was always speaking of God
being his strength, refuge, rock, stronghold, shield and high tower.
He knew where his high ground was.

In Psalm 27 he says that it was not Jerusalem (known as a military
fortress) that was his stronghold but God Himself,

"The Lord is my light and my salvation whom shall I fear? The Lord is the stronghold of my life of whom shall I be afraid?"

The Apostle Paul ends his letter to the Ephesians speaking about spiritual warfare but he begins it by telling them who they are in Christ and who He is in them. So before he tells them how to stand he shows them how they are already seated above all powers and principalities in the heavenly places.

This High Place is in what Jesus has done for us, shedding His blood and rising again from the grave. It is Jesus' victory over every power and principality of hell and forces of death.

On high ground we can more accurately discern the nature of the devil's strategy. Generally he either comes against a weakness or tries to wear us out. We can see whether the attack has been caused by our own selfishness and sinfulness or whether it is being allowed by God to mature us and train us for warfare.

Our victory is in Christ but preparation and
readiness is our responsibility.

How to Stand Against a Spiritual Attack

5

Develop Your Defences

If we lose our head in the battle we will
have no place to put our helmet

After the evacuation of British and French forces at Dunkirk in 1940 Britain stood alone against the might and conquest of the German Third Reich. The battle for Britain was about to begin. It would be fought not on land or sea but in the sky as the German Luftwaffe sought air supremacy to bring a huge armada of troop ships across the English Channel.

The defensive victory in 1940 at Dunkirk, which saved the British army, had frustrated German hopes of a swift end to the war in Western Europe and ensured that Britain remained a free and independent state able to carry on the war. Victory was eventually won in partnership with America and the Soviet Union, but without the retention of Britain's island base, it would have been impossible to launch the invasion for the liberation of Europe and achieve the eventual defeat of Nazi Germany.

On August 13 that year, Adlertag or "Eagle Day" the major Luftwaffe offensive began. British Fighter Command were outnumbered by more than two to one and were woefully short of trained pilots, yet the RAF not only stood against the German onslaught, they won a decisive victory that kept Britain free from invasion.

There were many factors in the British success but one of the most important and strategic was the development and deployment of radar which gave an accurate and early warning of the approach of German planes. By the spring of 1940, fifty-one radar bases had been built around the coast of southern Britain. There were also over 1000 Royal Observer Corps who used such basics as binoculars to do the same job. This gave the RAF a great advantage of knowing where, when and in what numbers the enemy was attacking and how to utilize its fighters to intercept them. Radar was the eyes of Fighter Command and thankfully in the 1930s Britain had developed its defensive warfare capability.

To stand and succeed against a spiritual attack we must develop and deploy our defensive systems. Demonic attacks in the spiritual realm are like bugs and germs in the natural one. There's a lot of harmful stuff out there but developing a strong and healthy spiritual immune system will keep us protected.

Discernment

Our spiritual radar is called discernment – it can help us to understand what is a spiritual attack, where it is coming from and how best to mobilize resources to deal with it.

In his book *The Devil's Gauntlet,* Os Guinness demonstrates Satan's cunning by relating a story told by Nikita Krushev about a time when there was an epidemic of petty theft in the Soviet Union. To curtail this the authorities put up guards around all the factories. At one factory in Leningrad the guards knew the workers well. The first evening out came Petrovich pushing a wheel barrow with a great stack on top of it with a suspicious looking object inside covered over.

"All right," said the guard, "What's inside the sack?" "Oh just sawdust shavings," Petrovich replied.

"Come on," said the guard, "I wasn't born yesterday, tip it out." He did and out came the contents of sawdust and shavings. He was allowed to put it all back and go home.

When the same thing happened every night of the week for the next two months the guard became frustrated. Finally, his curiosity overcame his frustration. "If you tell me what you are smuggling in those sacks I promise to let you go."

"I'm not smuggling anything inside the sacks," said Petrovich, "I'm smuggling wheel barrows, my friend, just wheel barrows."

The Greek word for discernment is *"diakrino,"* which means to make a judgment or a distinction. In 1 Corinthians 12:10 it is the divinely enabled ability to distinguish a good spirit from a bad spirit. It's not a function of the mind but of the Holy Spirit in union with your spirit. When the Holy Spirit sounds a warning, your mind may not be able to perceive what's wrong but your spirit is troubled and you sense all is not well.

There is a great hunger and desire among many believers for spiritual life and power. There is a longing for revival and while this is a good thing the danger is that people can become so hungry and thirsty they will eat and drink almost anything. This is why so many sincere Christians allow themselves to be deceived and can become very gullible. The writer A W Tozer said that the greatest gift we need in the church is the gift of discernment.

Spiritual discernment is not about judging people but discerning their spirit or a spirit that is working through them. This is why Jesus rebuked Peter when he tried to prevent Him from going to the cross, *"Get behind me Satan, for you do not have in mind the things of God but of man,"* Matthew 16:23. Jesus knew the spirit at work behind Peter.

Discerning often comes with a spiritual gut feeling and intuition that something is not right. There are many voices that claim to be from God and we have to test them all. We need to test everything by both the Word and the Spirit and must not be fooled by people's charisma and apparent success.

But a word of warning also for those who love to act as spiritual sheriffs, critical and cynical and eager to point out all that's wrong. Spiritual discernment is about seeking what is positive, not focusing on the negative,

> *Do not put out the Spirit's fire; do not treat prophecies with contempt. Test everything. Hold on to the good. Avoid every kind of evil.*

> 1 Thessalonians 5:19-22

This is important because we are naturally conditioned to have a prejudice for the negative. In other words we are more likely to examine something for the purpose of proving that it is false rather than confirming that it is true.

Peace

> *Do not be anxious about anything, but in everything, by prayer and petition, with thanksgiving, present your requests to God. And the peace of God, which transcends all understanding, will guard your hearts and your minds in Christ Jesus.*

> Philippians 4:6,7

The word *"guard"* Paul uses literally means to build a stockade or stronghold around. This is what Roman soldiers erected around their camps to protect themselves from surprise attacks. God builds a stronghold of peace around our hearts and minds as we pray with thanksgiving. Several years ago this truth became a lifesaver to me when I was very ill and feeling fragile and vulnerable. God spoke to me from this passage and I made sure that my prayers became filled with thanks. I made lists of all the things in my life to celebrate and praise God for. I made up songs and sang hymns filled with thanksgiving and worship. A proverb I had heard years before now became far more meaningful to me, "I complained I had no shoes until I met a man who had no feet." I had so many things in my life to be grateful for. I built a stronghold to guard my heart and mind from the enemy's attacks.

It's not what happens to us but what takes place within us that determines how we stand. We are never defeated until we are defeated on the inside.

Jesus prepared His disciples for warfare and warned them that in this world they would have tribulation, but to be of good cheer for He had overcome the world. In the hours before He was arrested He promised them His peace. *"My peace I leave with you; My peace I give to you; not as the world gives, do I give to you,"* John 14:27.

Smith Wigglesworth tells the story in his book *Ever Increasing Faith* how one night he was sleeping in a draughty room during a thunderstorm. The windows rattled, the lights flickered, and suddenly Wigglesworth saw a vision of Satan himself standing at the foot of his bed! But Wigglesworth was not in the least bit disturbed. He just dismissed the devil saying, "Oh, it's only you!" He then turned over in his bed and fell into a deep slumber God's peace enables us to rule in the midst of our enemies.

Humility

It's said that at a time of crisis during the American Civil War, Abraham Lincoln was awakened one night by an opportunist politician who reported that a member of Lincoln's closest staff had just died. "Mr President," he said, "Could I take his place?" "Well," said Lincoln, "if it's alright with the undertaker it's alright with me."

In his book *The Three Battle Grounds*, Francis Frangipane says,

> "We must recognise before we do warfare the areas we hide in darkness are the very areas of our future defeat. If we are to be effective in spiritual warfare, we must be discerning of our own hearts. We must walk humbly with God, for He cannot entrust His kingdom to those who have not been broken of pride, for pride is the armour of darkness itself. This is why Satan was given permission to sift Peter along with the disciples who had been arguing who was the greatest. Peter was ignorant of the darkness within him."

The devil hates humility. He cannot understand or comprehend it. When Paul appeals for unity within the churches he always encourages them to express humility because unity is impossible without it.

Even though the Romans as a nation became consumed by their pride, they still recognised its power to corrupt and destroy. Whenever there was a great military victory the returning general would lead a spectacular parade through the streets of Rome. Displayed were the conquered kings and nobles and the wagons of gold and treasures captured. The victorious general would ride at the head of his troops on a great carriage pulled by two white horses. Standing in the chariot behind the general stood a slave who held a laurel crown over the returning hero's head (not touching it). The slave had to repeat continuously "Memento mori", "remember thou art mortal." Some ancient sources state the slave would say "respica te hominem te memento", "Look behind you, you are only a man."

There is a story told about Muhammed Ali, voted the world's greatest sportsman of the 20th century. At the height of his boxing prowess and fame he was travelling across America by plane when he was asked by one stewardess to fasten his seat belt before take off. He quickly replied, "Superman don't need no seat belt." She smiled and said, "Sir, Superman don't need no airplane, please fasten your seat belt." He did.

Someone even more famous than Ali was not a sportsman or a politician but a preacher. Billy Graham has had a profound impact upon our world. He is the friend and confident of presidents and kings. In 1955 he held an evangelistic crusade in Great Britain but many in the country looked at his trip to "save" them with anger and contempt. Newspaper reporters were especially hostile. They openly harassed him at the port when he arrived. He describes in his autobiography, *Just As I Am*, the hostility, "Would Jesus travel on a luxury liner?" scoffed a reporter. "Do you really think you can save England?" sneered another. "Just how much money do you plan to haul out of England?" needled another reporter.

The crusade was a tremendous success but the press remained unrelentingly hostile. A proud man would have fumed under the unfair attack but Graham determined to meet as many of the press as possible. His goodness and humility melted them one by one. One *Daily Express* columnist admitted he goaded Billy unmercifully during an interview. But suddenly he was overwhelmed by the realization, "He is a good man. I am not sure he isn't a saintly man...But make no mistake about this. Billy Graham is a remarkable man...it is a bitter pill to swallow...(after Graham left me) my eyes were scalding with tears."

The most vicious attacker was a journalist who wrote for the *Daily Mirror* known as "Cassandra." In polite letters Billy asked again and again to meet with him. Finally Cassandra agreed – if Billy would meet him in a particularly nasty pub where every other word uttered was a swear word. He was sure Billy would not show up. But he did.

Days later "Cassandra" wrote in his column,

> "(Billy Graham has) a kind of ferocious cordiality that scares ordinary sinners stone cold...He came into the Baptist's Head (pub) absolutely at home – a teetotaler and an abstainer able to make himself completely at home in the spit and sawdust... a difficult thing to do. I never thought that friendliness had such a sharp cutting edge. I never thought that simplicity could cudgel us sinners so (expletive deleted) hard. We live and learn...The bloke means everything he says..."

When Billy finally returned to America the British press was friendly, even sorry to see him go. He had won them over not with intelligence or charm but with humility born of love.

6

Attack Your Attacker

David ran towards Goliath
1 Samuel 17:48

The old boxing maxim says "the best form of defence is attack." That may be true but only if you have got a good attack.

Two of the greatest dangers we face in battle are those of defeatism at the one extreme and triumphalism at the other. Both can be equally dangerous. Defeatism comes in many guises, through fear like the ten spies who persuaded the Israelites they could not possess the Promised Land. What should have been an eleven day journey took 40 years and more than a million deaths. Through discouragement, like Elijah who ran from Jezebel into the wilderness and sat under a juniper tree and wanted to die. Through disappointment and loss of hope like the two disciples on the Emmaus Road (Luke 24).

Triumphalism on the other hand is perhaps even more dangerous, as it underestimates the enemy and makes unwise decisions. The Charge of the Light Brigade in 1854 during the Crimean War between British and Russian forces is a classic and tragic example, it was an act of unfathomable stupidity. It's been said that the sheer stupidity of the commanders increased in direct proportion to their rank.

The British Lieutenant-General, the Earl of Cardigan, ordered his light brigade to attack the Russian artillery positions ("light" because they were lightly armed, as opposed to the "heavy brigade"). Success was impossible. The charge was through a narrow valley a mile and a quarter long. Russian guns were at the end of the valley and gunners were on both sides, forming a death box. The whole thing took about 20 minutes and though the brigade was not completely destroyed, it suffered terribly. After regrouping, only 195 men out of more than an initial 600 were still with horses. The futility of the action and its reckless bravery prompted the French Marshal Pierre Bosquet to make the much quoted observation, "C'est magnifique, mais ce n'est pas la guerre," (It is magnificent, but it is not war). He continued, in a rarely quoted phrase, "C'est de la folie" – it is madness.

When the devil attacks us we need to realise that this is an opportunity for us to attack him and his kingdom for he has revealed himself and his plans. We once bought a house in a lovely location but the garden had become a jungle. I spent weeks digging up weeds and roots and turning over the soil. It looked lovely but after a few more weeks all the weeds I had missed started to come up through the ground. They looked horrible, like some insidious alien invasion on my recently cultivated lawn. But this was also my opportunity to finally rid the garden of them. They had shown where they were and I could dig them up and deal with them.

When we are attacked with lust we can use it to drive us to God and pray for the people we are tempted with and intercede for those bound by sexual bondage and pornography. If we are continually susceptible to it and bombarded by it we can also examine ourselves to make sure that a "stronghold" of sexual impurity has not taken hold in our lives. If we are attacked by greed we can recognise our dependence on God who has promised to meet all our needs and we can repent of any hold the power of money has in our lives. When envy is used to assail us we can repent over any jealous traits we have and pray for God to bless those we have been jealous of. When the enemy shows himself he makes himself vulnerable.

The Name of Jesus

The Early Church didn't preach a creed or a religion but went everywhere and spoke about Jesus. They healed the sick in His name, they baptised in His name, raised the dead in His name, cast out demons in His name. When they were warned not to teach and preach or mention that name, they proclaimed, *"Salvation is found in no one else for there is no other name under heaven given to men where by we must be saved,"* (Acts 4:12).

The devil is not impressed by our titles, reputation or status. Demons do not tremble because of what others call us or by what we call ourselves. It is not our name or title they fear but Jesus.

We must also understand that there is a great difference between ministering and praying *with* the name of Jesus to ministering and praying *in* the name of Jesus. His "name" is not meant to be used as a *formula* of Him but is a *fellowship* with Him. It was never meant to be used as a mantra of religious repetition but as an expression of our union with Him by the presence and power of the Holy Spirit. We read in Acts 19:13-17 about the seven sons of Sceva, a Jewish Chief Priest, who went around trying to invoke the name of Jesus over those who were demonically possessed. On this occasion an evil spirit answered them and said it knew of Jesus but questioned who were they? They had no authority whatever name they were using. The man who had the evil spirit jumped on them and beat them so badly they fled the place naked.

The Word of God

A Bible Society survey in the UK revealed that in an average church of 50 people, only ten per cent read the Bible every day and only 30 per cent read it at all between Sundays! It's amazing how many people believe the Bible is the most important book in the world yet they have never read it all the way through.

When I was in Bible College a visiting speaker challenged me profoundly when he told the story of a preacher who asked his listeners, "How many believe all you read in the newspapers? Please lift your hand." No one did. Then he asked, "How many believe all you hear on the radio?" There was a similar response. Finally he asked, "How many of you believe the Bible to be the word of God?" There was a unanimous response. But he wasn't finished as he then added, "How many spend more time in the things you don't believe that with the things you do believe?"

One of the most quoted scriptures regarding spiritual warfare is found in Isaiah 10:27, *"And the yoke shall be destroyed because of the anointing," (King James translation)*. More recent versions say the yoke of bondage will be broken because *"of fatness"* or *"because you have grown so fat."* The word used here for anointing implies growth and strength causing the increase of power to destroy every attack and bondage of the enemy. One of the most recognised and definitive commentaries on the Old Testament is that of Keil and Delitzsch which says *"...the yoke, like the burden, will be taken away from Israel; that yoke itself will snap from the pressure of his fat strong neck against it..."* In other words, God will strengthen the Israelites, and the yoke that Assyria tries to put on them will not fit. When the bondage of the enemy seeks to bind them it will utterly fail.

Sometimes the impression is given that all we need to have to break free and live free from spiritual bondage is something (anointing) come upon us. But this verse actually teaches that God's life needs to well up within us and because of the "fatness" of spiritual growth and blessing the yoke will be totally destroyed. The great healing evangelist Smith Wigglesworth used to say, "I am 100 times bigger on the inside than I look on the outside." He was a man of the Spirit who loved the word of God, and who fellowshipped with Him in prayer and through life. This is where the power of the anointing came from in his ministry.

I like the story of a woman who bought a parrot, took him home, and then returned him to the pet shop the next day. "This bird doesn't talk," she told the owner. "Does he have a mirror?" he asked. "Parrots love mirrors. They see themselves and start up a conversation." So the woman bought a mirror. Next day she returned. The bird still wasn't talking. "How about a ladder?" enquired the store's owner. "Parrots love walking up and down a ladder. A happy parrot is more likely to talk." The woman bought a ladder. Sure enough, she was back the next day; the bird still wasn't talking. "Does your parrot have a swing? If not, that's the problem. He'll relax and talk no end," she was told. The woman reluctantly bought a swing and left.

When she walked into the shop the next day her countenance had changed. "The parrot died," she said. The pet shop owner was shocked. "I'm so sorry. Tell me, did he ever say a word?" he asked. "Yes, right before he died," the woman replied. "He said, 'Don't they sell any food at that pet shop?'"

We can spend our whole life looking at mirrors, focusing on appearance, climbing ladders, focusing on career success, swinging on swings and living for entertainment and yet in the process starve to death spiritually and emotionally.

When Jesus was tempted in the wilderness, each time He countered the devil's attack by quoting the Word of God, but it was specific and revalent to the particular temptation. Finally, Jesus attacked His attacker and commanded, *"Away from me, Satan! For it is written: 'Worship the Lord your God, and serve him only,'"* Matthew 4:10.

"The sword of the spirit" mentioned in Ephesians 6 is an awesome weapon. It refers to not only knowing the Bible but being able to apply its truth to a specific situation. The *"Belt of Truth"* is the Word of God, the sword is drawn from the belt – it is a "word" from the Word in the power of the Holy Spirit.

Lord Admiral Nelson was a great admiral and national hero. He is most famous for his victory over the French at the Battle of Trafalgar in 1805. It's said that twice daily for most of his life, he studied and recorded the weather – what the wind, waves, swell and temperature were doing. He did so whether on land or at sea. There came a moment in the Battle of Trafalgar when all the years of disciplined study and recording the weather proved vital. Nelson drew on his reservoir of experience and knowledge as he noticed that a change in the swell of the sea pointed to an advancing storm days before it broke. Instead of having a conventional battle where the two lines of ships lined up against each other in parallel, he seized the advantage offered by the conditions to slice through and destroy the enemy armada. His daily discipline gave him the experience and confidence to make a decisive judgement at a critical time.

The Power of Jesus' Blood

Someone once asked Corrie ten Boom her opinion of missionaries in a certain country. She remarked that they had given all but they had not taken all. They had given up homeland, time, money, luxury and more but they had not taken all the boundless resources of God's promises, many did not know about the precious weapons of the name of Jesus and the power of the blood of Jesus.

In her book *Tramp for the Lord,* she shared some of the spiritual attacks that came against her as she travelled around to minister,

> "In Warsaw one day we happened to meet an old friend from Holland 'What a joy to meet you,' said Kees, 'how are things going?' I looked at Conny (my travelling companion) and she at me. 'You know Kees we both feel so tired. It is as if our legs are heavy like when you have the flu yet we are not ill just tired.' Kees looked at me intently, 'Is this your first time to work in Poland?' 'Yes,' I answered, 'but what does that have to do with it?'

> "'Let me explain,' said Kees, 'your tiredness is nothing less than an attack of the devil, he does not like your work in Poland for the antichrist is busy here arranging his army.' Reaching out he put his hand on my arm and said to us, 'Remember you must remember you have the protection of the blood of Jesus. Whenever you experience these attacks from dark powers you must rebuke them in the name of Jesus.'

"I knew what Kees was saying was right but we sat in his car while he read from the Bible, '*they overcame him by the blood of the lamb and by the word of their testimony and they loved not their lives unto death.*'

"Then Kees laid his hands on us and in the name of Jesus rebuked the dark powers that would attack us. Even as he was praying I felt the powers of darkness leave, by the time he had finished praying we both felt covered by the blood of the Lamb and all our tiredness disappeared.

"God had taught us while ministering that only by claiming the blood of Jesus can you stand and not fall. If Jesus is not recognised as supreme then darkness reigns. Since then we have travelled to many countries and felt this same tiredness coming over us, often in American cities. Now I know it simply means I am in a place where Satan rules but praise the Lord I can be an overcomer when I stand in the power of the blood of the lamb."

Blood symbolises both death and life in scripture and Jesus' blood speaks of the power of His cross and resurrection.

The evangelist Reinhard Bonke tells how he was taking part in a televised debate with an atheist who made the comment, "If the blood of Jesus is supposed to be so powerful, why is there so much evil in the world?" Bonke replied, "You can work in a soap factory and still stink!"

The power of Jesus' blood becomes effective for us when we apply it by faith and confession.

Songs of Deliverance

*You will protect me from trouble and surround me with **songs of deliverance.***

Psalm 32:7

Moody Monthly magazine carried the following story. When the American singer/songwriter Ira Sankey was at the height of his ministry, while travelling on a steamer in the Delaware River, he was recognized by some of the passengers. They'd seen his picture in the newspaper and knew he was associated with the evangelist D. L. Moody. When they asked him to sing one of his compositions, Sankey said he preferred to sing the hymn by William Bradbury, *Saviour, Like a Shepherd Lead Us.* He suggested that everyone join in the singing. One of the stanzas begins, "We are thine, do thou befriend us; be the guardian of our way."

When he finished, a man stepped out of the shadows and inquired, "Were you in the army, Mr Sankey?" "Yes, I joined up in 1860." "Did you ever do guard duty at night in Maryland, about 1862?" "Yes, I did." "Well, I was in the Confederate Army," said the stranger. "I saw you one night at Sharpsburg. I had you in my gun sight as you stood there in the light of the full moon. Then just as I was about to pull the trigger, you began to sing. It was the same hymn you sang tonight," the man told an astonished Sankey. "I couldn't shoot you."

In 2 Chronicles 20 we see a godly king, Jehoshaphat, being confronted by a vast army intent on destroying his kingdom. Greatly outnumbered he turns to God and all the people humble themselves in worship. They are told,

*You will not have to fight this battle. Take up your positions; **stand firm and see the deliverance the***

71

Lord will give you, O Judah and Jerusalem. Do not be afraid; do not be discouraged. Go out to face them tomorrow, and the Lord will be with you.

2 Chronicles 20:17

The next day as they march out to fight, Jehoshaphat appoints men to sing to the Lord at the head of the army, *"Give thanks to the Lord for His love endures forever."* As they praise and worship, God fights for them and sets ambushes against the invading army who are thrown into confusion and slaughter each other

Songs of deliverance can be a hymn, a chorus, a scripture, a Psalm, an old song or a new song that God uses to bring peace and deliverance even in the midst of severe trials. As you sing them over your life faith starts to rise. They are songs that break the power of the oppressor by bringing the presence of God. As you put on the garments of praise the spirit of heaviness has to leave, Isaiah 61:3.

7

The Armour of God

*When we kneel before God we can
stand against anything*

When flying at high altitude above the clouds one would expect a smooth flight but as any frequent flyer will tell you there come those scary moments when the plane hits rough air. The little red light goes on to fasten your seat belt and the pilot says over the intercom, "We are encountering some turbulence." Everything is usually fine until you see the stewardesses looking worried and you remember that when you left the airport you boarded the plane from something called a "terminal."

Here are some of my favourite pilot jokes,

*   While flying in a propeller plane, the passengers saw three of the four engines suddenly stop. The cockpit door opened and the pilot appeared with a parachute on his back, saying, "Keep calm, folks, and don't panic, I'm going for help!

*   A passenger in a commuter plane was amazed when the pilot began to laugh uncontrollably during the flight. "What's so funny?" asked the passenger. "I'm thinking of what they will say at the asylum when they find out I have escaped," said the pilot.

*   After a really bad landing the pilot had to stand at the door and thank the passengers for travelling with his airline. Finally everyone had left except for one little old lady walking with a cane. She said, "Sonny, mind if I ask you a question?" "Why no Ma'am," said the pilot, "What is it?" The little old lady asked, "Did we land or were we shot down?"

At the end of his letter to the Ephesians Paul reminds us that even when living at high altitude and being seated with Christ in heavenly places we can still experience spiritual turbulence. We not only have a God who loves us but fight against a devil who hates us.

God's Armour

Ephesians 6 comes at the end of the book not at the beginning for very good reasons – our foundations and focus have to be in Christ before we can effectively fight and overcome the devil. It is not the devil who defeats us but our openness to him. He is not frightened of us but by Jesus who is within us. It is becoming more like Jesus and being filled with God's Spirit that defeats Satan.

i)   As we have already stated Satan and his demons are not in hell but in the heavenly realms, the fallen moral and spiritual realm that is all around us.

ii)   There is no armour for the back. It is extremely dangerous to turn your back on your enemy. A backslidden Christian is a spiritually defeated one.

iii)   We must put on the *whole armour.* Any chink in our defences will be exploited. It is not enough to say you love God's truth (the belt) if you are not living in righteousness (the breastplate).

iv)   Every piece of the armour has a reference to Jesus. He is our peace, righteousness, truth, faith, hope, salvation, the living Word of God. So the call to get dressed for battle is the need to put on the person of Christ. It is the whole armour of God and Jesus is God.

v)   Paul tells us that the devil attacks with three basic battle plans – through *surprise,* with fiery darts, through *subtly,* with his wiles and cunning and through *siege,* the evil day.

Tom Marshall in his book which I have already quoted, points out the Greek word *"panoplia"* meaning *whole armour,* is used twice in the New Testament, once in Ephesians 6 and once in Luke 11:22, *"When a strong man **fully armed** keeps his household, everything is at peace."* Jesus is saying the devil has a full armour which is a set of life conditions that he wants to establish in you and when they take hold they enable him to work. The armour of God is also a set of life conditions and spiritual characteristics that He wants to establish within us. It doesn't matter how much we quote the armour as protection, if we don't live and walk in God's provision and purpose we are vulnerable.

God's Life Conditions

Truth *Stand firm then, with the belt of truth buckled around your waist.*

Ephesians 6:14

The book *The Day America Told The Truth* reported that 91 per cent of those interviewed admit that they lie regularly. In the United Kingdom *The National Scruples and Lies Survey* in 2004 quizzed 5,000 women. It found 96 per cent lie about everything from how good their lover is to stealing from friends. And most don't even feel guilty about it.

The first piece of armour Paul mentions is *"the belt of truth"* which holds the rest of the armour together. Satan cannot stand against truth because there is no truth in him. We are told *"he is a liar, and the father of lies,"* (John 8:44). Therefore overcoming demonic powers is firstly a truth encounter (light shines into the darkness) and following that a power encounter can take place. This is why Jesus said, *"You shall know the truth, and the truth shall make you free"* (John 8:32).

Righteousness *With the breastplate of righteousness in place.*

Ephesians 6:14

The breastplate is God's righteousness which is given to us in Christ but we have to put it on by our desire to live righteously. The breastplate covered the vital organs which were the primary target of the enemy in battle.

Charles Spurgeon, the nineteenth century English preacher, gave the following counsel to his students training for ministry,

"Every workman knows the necessity of keeping his tools in a good state of repair. If the workman loses the edge he knows that there will be a greater draw upon his energy, or his work will be badly done. It will be vain for me to stock my library, or organise societies, or project schemes, if I neglect the culture of myself: for books and agencies and systems are only remotely the instruments of my holy calling. My own spirit, soul and body are my nearest machinery for sacred service, my spiritual faculties and my inner life are my battle axe and weapons for war.

(Then quoting from a letter of the great Scottish minister, Robert Murray McCheyne he concludes)

"Remember you are God's sword, instrument, I trust a chosen vessel unto Him to bear His Name. In great measure, according to the purity and perfection of the instrument, will be the success. It is not great talent God blesses so much as likeness to Jesus. A holy minister is an awful weapon in the hands of God."

Peace   *...and with your feet fitted with the readiness that comes from the gospel of peace.*

Ephesians 6:15

Roman soldiers wore heavy sandals with studs in the soles to give them swift mobility and stability. When we lose our peace we become unstable and vulnerable. Instead of faith and confidence, doubt and confusion mean we are "all over the place."

Faith and Trust   *In addition to all this, take up the shield of faith, with which you can extinguish all the flaming arrows of the evil one.*

Ephesians 6:16

Faith is the ability to trust and lay hold of God's promises, unlike the man who fell from a high cliff. Hanging on by a branch half way down he cries out, "Is anybody there?" A voice answers, "Yes, I am here." "Who are you?" shouts the man. "I am God," says the voice. "What shall I do?" the frantic faller asks. The voice answers, "Let go of the branch and trust me." A few seconds later the man shouts out again, "Is there anybody else there?"

There were two kinds of shields used by Roman soldiers. One was small and round and the other was heavy and oblong, which heavily armoured soldiers used. It is the large, heavy shield Paul is referring to here. It was used to combat one of the most dangerous weapons in ancient warfare – the fiery dart dipped in pitch. The shield therefore was made of a wood that when the arrow sank into it the flame would be extinguished.

Hope   *Take the helmet of salvation.*

Ephesians 6:17

Putting on the hope of salvation as a helmet.

1 Thessalonians 5:8

The devil destroys hope because hopelessness is the crucible in which he will grind you down and wear you out. We are never defeated until we are defeated on the inside and this usually comes with the loss of hope. When our hope is gone so is our faith, *"Faith is the substance of things hoped for,"* Hebrews 11:1.

78

The helmet of salvation protects our minds. It is the knowledge of who Jesus is and what He has done for us. Some of the fiercest battles we fight are in the mind. Invariably they are private battles because we do not want others to know what goes on there. Ten of the fifteen works of the flesh mentioned in Galatians have to do with our thought lives.

How do we determine if the thoughts are from within ourselves or if they are a spiritual attack against us? Dr Martyn Lloyd Jones offers the following wise advice on this matter,

> "If the thought that comes is something you hate and detest and it takes you unawares and comes out of the blue and you refuse to linger over it, then it is most likely a spiritual attack. But if the thought comes out of what you enjoy reading and watching and you drool over it then it most likely comes from within."

An ungodly thought from without needs to be rebuked and one from within must be repented of.

The Word and Prayer   *Taking the sword of the Spirit, which is the word of God. And pray in the Spirit on all occasions with all kinds of prayers and requests. With this in mind, be alert and always keep on praying for all the saints.*

Ephesians 6:18

The sword of the Spirit is the weapon we pull from the "*belt of truth*" which is the Bible. It is the word taken from the Word that is specifically relevant to be applied as we are led and directed by the Holy Spirit.

Paul concludes by saying that all of this armour and warfare has to be enveloped with prayer and the power of the Holy Spirit. It is not something mechanical and formulistic but is part of a living dynamic relationship with Christ.

8

Overcoming Temptation

Forbidden fruits create frightful jams

I can govern my people, but how can I govern myself?
Peter the Great of Russia

There was a very large lady who was determined to start to lose weight and the first two days of her diet went well. The problem was that each day on her way to work she had to pass her favourite cake shop. On the third day she went into the office and her colleagues, who were supporting her in the effort to lose weight, were horrified to see she had brought in a huge chocolate cake to eat for her coffee break. She assured them God wanted her to have it as she had prayed asking Him to provide a car space right outside the cake shop if it was His will. Sure enough she said, on the 37th time around the block the car space was empty.

It's amazing what you can persuade yourself is right if you want something badly enough whether it is a piece of cake or a one night stand. The problem is *"the heart is deceitful above all things,"* Jeremiah 17:9. One of the most important ways of overcoming temptation is to be honest with yourself and with God.

81

Unlike the person who tried to explain away his responsibility for breaking the law and received double punishment. He said to the judge, "Your Honour, as a believer in Christ I am a 'new man,' but I still have an old nature, and it was the 'old man' that committed the crime." The judge's reply to his plea was, "Since it was the 'old man' that broke the law, we'll sentence him to 30 days in jail. And since the 'new man' was an accomplice in the wrong, we'll also give him 30 days. I therefore sentence you to jail for 60 days!"

There's also the story of the young child who was in a very bad mood. She took her frustration out on her younger brother, at first just teasing him, but eventually punching him pulling his hair and kicking him in the shins. He went crying to his mother who asked his sister, "Mary, why did you do that?" She answered, "The devil made me do it." Her mother said, "Is that completely true?" The little girl thought for a moment and answered, "Well, maybe the devil did make me punch him but pulling his hair and kicking his shins was my idea."

In her book *The Hiding Place*, Corrie ten Boom made a profound observation about the futility of rationalizing our sins when she wrote, "The blood of Jesus never cleansed an excuse."

One church member said to her pastor, "I'm deeply troubled about a problem I know is hurting my testimony, I exaggerate. I always seem to enlarge a story until it's all distorted. People know they can't trust me. Can you help me?" The minister said, "Let's talk to the Lord about it." She began to pray, "O God, you know I have a tendency to exaggerate..." At this point her pastor interrupted, "Call it lying, ma'am, and you may get over it!"

Understanding Temptation

> *When tempted, no one should say, "God is tempting me." For God cannot be tempted by evil, nor does he tempt anyone; but each one is tempted when, by his own evil desire (lust), he is dragged away and enticed. Then, after desire has conceived, it gives birth to sin; and sin, when it is full-grown, gives birth to death.*
>
> James 1:13-15

Temptation is not sin. Jesus was tempted relentlessly (Mark 1:13) in the wilderness and remained pure. Neither does God tempt us. He will test us at times but this is totally different. Testing is to strengthen us to stand against sin while temptation is to get us to yield to it. So why does God test us and allow temptation? The answer is to give us an opportunity to grow. Every time you choose to do right instead of wrong, you are growing in the character of Christ.

James tells us that though temptation is common to all each one of us is uniquely susceptible to different temptations. We individually have a propensity to a particular path and type of sin. What affects others may not bother you in the slightest but equally the temptation that most affects you may be something that is not the least problem to someone else, *"Each one is tempted, by his own evil desire."* Different factors and life experiences have contributed to our spiritual DNA and its inbuilt weaknesses against and desire for certain sinful desires. Isaiah graphically points this out when he says, *"Everyone has turned to his **own** way,"* Isaiah 53:6.

Temptation is therefore general to all but lust (a particular sin) is specific shaped to the continuity of our own individual, spiritual, emotional and psychological profile.

Jesus was tempted in all things but could say, *"the prince of this world is coming but he has nothing in me,"* John 14:30. For the devil to succeed against you he has to come against something he has within you. It's not what happens to us but what occurs within us that causes us to give in to temptation. We need to ask ourselves, "Why am I so vulnerable to that particular sin? Is there a stronghold of unrighteousness that needs to be demolished?"

The devil will come against us with tailor made packages. With Judas it was money, with Samson it was women, with Demas it was the love of the world, with Simon Magus it was his desire for power, with David it was a beautiful woman and so the list goes on.

Screwtape and Temptation

In his book *The Screwtape Letters,* C S Lewis describes the work of a senior devil named Screwtape as he instructs a junior devil named Wormwood in the art of temptation. Both are in the civil service of hell, charged with tempting humans. The format of the book is a collection of 31 letters from Screwtape to his nephew Wormwood, with each sharing techniques on how Wormwood can derail the Christian faith of his patient, a 20-something-year-old British man living during World War II.

The idea for the book has its roots in a radio speech made by Adolph Hitler that Lewis heard in July of 1940. Lewis was struck by the speech's impact on him, and in writing to his brother Warnie, he confessed that he found it impossible not to waver slightly in his thinking in the midst of the speech. Lewis added, "Statements which I know to be untrue all but convince me... for the moment, if only the man says them unflinchingly."

The next day, as he was sitting in a Communion service, Lewis reflected on how Satan's temptations are much like Hitler's persuasive power. In other words, Satan can twist reality and truth into something you know to be false, yet you still get sucked into believing it. And so Lewis began to consider how this premise could be turned into a book. One of the key ideas of the project was to look at the world from Satan's point of view. Therefore the book is full of opposites: Bad is good, good is bad, God is the enemy and hell becomes "Our Father's House."

The focus of the letters is the spiritual battle that takes place, the events of the person's life are only important insofar as they impact on his spiritual life. Lewis provides insight into the techniques that Satan uses to tempt and trap people and his book reveals five actions that the devil uses to take advantage of us.

Denying and disguising the spiritual world

Lewis believes the devil is most effective when he gets people to deny the reality of the spiritual world. In this light Screwtape gets Wormwood to focus the patient on the physical material world around him. The idea is that the more real the physical world is, the less real the spiritual world becomes. He advises, "Your business is to fix your attention on the stream (of immediate sense experiences). Teach him to call it real life and don't let him ask what he means by real."

The power of materialism is that it blinds people to the spiritual realm and spiritual realities. The more material you become the less spiritual your life.

Satan holds out the world as the prize

Not only does Satan want to deny the reality of the spiritual realm, but he also wants people to invest their hearts and minds in this current world. In Letter 23 Screwtape writes, "Make men treat Christianity as a means, preferably of course, as a means to their own advancement, but failing that as a means to anything." He tells Wormwood to guide his patient to believe Christianity not because it is true, but for some other reason – that is the game.

Satan doesn't want people to think clearly

Lewis doesn't believe the devil has the power to control or change people's thoughts but he will do everything to stop them thinking clearly and influence them. He believes that if they look at reality with a clear and level mind Satan will always lose and that is why he does all in his power to distract them.

Jesus said, it was when the Prodigal Son came to his senses he decided to go back home to his father's house.

Satan distracts with fashion

The kind of fashion Lewis refers to is not the latest clothes styles but whatever is hip and popular. Satan ensures people are never content with who they are or who they're married to. Lewis believes fashion, the popular view of society, will always look down upon traditional orthodox Christianity.

Lewis believes the devil can't prevent people from believing in Christianity but he tempts humans to water down their faith with fashion. In Letter 25 Screwtape says, "Substitute for the faith itself some fashion with a Christian colouring." In other words, Satan waters down Christianity by using faith as the means to another end, such as politics, world hunger, abortion etc. All these are important but they become the main focus instead of Jesus.

Satan uses monotony as a weapon

Screwtape writes, "The horror of the same old thing is one of the most valuable passions we have produced in the human heart – an endless source of heresies in religion, folly in counsel, infidelity in marriage."

Snares of the Tempter

Imagine four steel rings. The first can support up to 80 pounds in weight, the second 60 pounds, the third 40 and the fourth 20. Linked together what's the greatest weight the chain can support? Two hundred pounds? No! A chain is only as strong as its weakest link, so the answer is 20 pounds. When it comes to temptation we too are only as strong as our weakest point.

There are basically three channels through which temptation comes. John tells us,

> *For all that is in the world, the lust of the flesh and the lust of the eyes and the boastful pride of life, is not from the Father, but is from the world.*

> 1 John 2:16

Temptation always focuses on self gratification, self promotion and self exaltation. Lust is the desire to get which is the opposite of love which is the desire to give.

In Genesis 3 the serpent tempted Eve in exactly this way,

> *When the woman saw that the tree was good for food (**lust of the flesh)**, and that it was a delight*

> *to the eyes (**lust of the eyes**), and that the tree was*
> *desirable to make one wise (**pride of life**), she*
> *took from its fruit and ate.*
>
> Genesis 3:6

Adam and Eve ate the forbidden fruit and it turned out, as God had warned, to be the most expensive meal in history. Someone has said they literally ate mankind out of house and home and we are still picking up the bill.

Jesus was tempted in the wilderness to *"turn stones into bread,"* Matthew 4:3. (The lust of the flesh – self gratification). This temptation was, as James warns, particularly targeted to where we are most susceptible at that moment. Jesus was physically hungry after being without food for forty days. The second temptation was for Jesus to prove to Himself and others that He really was the Messiah, God's Son, by throwing Himself from the top of the Temple so angels would come and protect Him. (The pride of life – self promotion). When this also failed Jesus was shown and offered all the kingdoms of the world if He would bow down and worship him, Satan. (The lust of the eyes – self exaltation).

The devil doesn't mind what you have so long as he has you because then he has everything you have as well. When I was a young boy I was fascinated by the game Monopoly where players travel around a game board buying property and trying to bankrupt the other players to win. I used to play my grandfather who didn't know the game very well and so I let him have almost all the money on the condition that I had all the property. He had the cash but I owned the board and it wasn't long before I had the cash as well as in the course of the game he kept landing on my properties and had to pay me rent. When the devil offered Jesus all the kingdoms of world he was giving nothing away.

Where the first Adam failed, Christ the Second Adam overcame and in Him we have all the resources and power to conquer every temptation Satan throws at us,

> *No temptation has overtaken you but such as is common to man; and God is faithful, who will not allow you to be tempted beyond what you are able, but with the temptation will provide the way of escape also, that you may be able to endure it.*

1 Corinthians 10:13

Walk in the Light

The devil hates spiritual and moral light, he cannot come into it to ensnare you so what he does is to allure you and tempt you into the darkness where he is. This is his ultimate goal in all temptation. It is not simply to cause us to sin but to bring us into his domain which the Bible calls "bondage." The devil can never defeat us unless we open our lives to him.

I often illustrate this in a dramatized way. I ask for a group of people to come and stand at the front of the audience and make a circle joining hands. I have someone stand in the centre and explain that this circle represents God's light and protection for them. I myself illustrate how the devil comes against the one in the centre of the circle by trying to break into the circle, but unsuccessfully. I shout from the outside but there is no way in. So what I do is stand just outside and try and tempt the one inside to come out of the circle. I hold up my hands for the person to touch and even though the person's feet and body are inside the enclosed circle there is part of them that now ventures near the edge and reaches outside. After a short time the person inside is slapping hands with "the devil" and the circle begins to break apart as the person inside is lured slowly but surely outside at which point I drag them away and run off with them! It usually draws a lot of laughs but the seriousness of what has happened has a powerful impact. Being drawn to the outer edge of the circle and putting your hands outside is what temptation seeks to achieve. Most of you may be inside but some part of you reaches out from within and you become compromised and vulnerable.

I refer to this as "roaming in the gloaming." I lived and ministered for 15 years in Scotland where this expression is very popular. The gloaming refers to that time of day between light and darkness. It's a murky light and for some people can make things seem a little unreal. I know Biblically that spiritually and morally light and darkness are clearly defined. Yet what most Christians have a problem with is not the darkness but the "gloaming" where they stand in the circle but put their hands outside. We may not be living in the darkness of adultery but still live at the edge of the circle and experience what Lord Byron, the English poet, referred to as, "not quite adultery, but adulteration."

The Christian author David Seamands says about this, "I'm intrigued by the words of Jesus, '*watch and pray lest you enter into temptation.*' He doesn't say lest you enter into sin. That's always fascinated me. I suspect He chose His words carefully because He knew that some temptations, including sexual attraction, are so powerful that after a certain point, the will gives into the urge. It's like a toboggan down a hill – once it gets going it's almost impossible to stop."

When John Wesley left home and went to study at Oxford University he met temptations he had never encountered before and he was unsure if things such as cards, gambling, dancing and going to the theatre were sinful. So he wrote home for advice to his beloved mother Susannah, from whom he said he learned more about God than all the theologians in England. This was her reply,

> "Dear John, If you would judge of the lawfulness or the unlawfulness of pleasure, take this rule, whatever weakens your reason, impairs the tenderness of your conscience, obscures your sense of God, or takes off your relish of spiritual things; in short, whatever increases the strength and authority of your body over your mind, that thing is sin to you, however innocent it may be in itself."

Walk in the Spirit

> *So I say, walk in the Spirit, and you will not gratify the desires of the sinful nature.*
>
> Galatians 5:16

The devil is the tempter, the world is the temptation and the flesh is always the tempted. The flesh is our selfish will and desires, our ungodly thought processes and thinking patterns.

I heard an interesting fact that illustrates this perfectly. During autumn trees start shedding their leaves and for a time can look quite bare, while a tree that has been cut down lying on the ground will continue to have leaves for much longer. The reason is that leaves don't fall off trees – they are pushed off by the life of the sap rising within to produce new ones. This is why dead trees may still have their leaves while live ones shed theirs. But we all know there comes a time when the dead tree and its leaves will rot and decay. When the life of God's Spirit is flowing within us we are empowered to live godly lives. In fact we cannot do it without Him, our part is to cooperate. We know we are doing this, not by living with endless lists of do's and don'ts but by the desire to be more like Jesus. He is to be our focus not the enemy or ourselves. I love the words of Robert Murray McCheyne who said, "For every one look I take at myself, I take ten looks at Jesus."

9

Overcoming Fear

*"How can I get past the pain?" the late Michael
Jackson once asked an associate. "I'm so tired of
being controlled by fear."*

*The greatest enemy a human being can take into
his life is fear. If you are able to conquer the
enemy of fear, you have come a long way
to bring health to a physical body.*
Kathryn Kuhlman

An emergency operator received a call one evening but there was
no voice at the other end. Extremely concerned, the operator called
back, and a little boy answered the phone in a whispering voice...
[barely audible] "Hello!"
(Operator) "Hello little boy. Did you just call 999?"
[barely audible] "No!"
(Operator) OK, is your mummy home?"
[barely audible] "Yes."
(Operator) "Can I speak to her, please?"
[barely audible] "No."
(Operator) "Why not?"

[barely audible] "Because she's busy!"
(Operator) "Oh, OK. Is your daddy home then?"
[barely audible] "Yes."
(Operator) "Well, can I speak to him?"
[barely audible] "No!"
(Operator) "Well, my goodness, why not?"
[barely audible] "Because he's busy too!"
(Operator) "Oh, goodness! What's he busy doing?"
[barely audible] "Talking to the police."
(Operator) "Oh, so the police are there?"
[barely audible] "Yes."
(Operator) "Can I speak to one of them?"
[barely audible] "No!"
(Operator) "Why not?"
[barely audible] "Because they are really busy."
(Operator) "Well, what's your mum busy doing?"
[barely audible] "Talking to the firemen."
(Operator) "Can I speak to one of the firemen then, please?"
[barely audible] "No."
(Operator) "Well, goodness, why not?"
[barely audible] "Because they are really busy too!"
(Operator) "Well, what are all of these people busy doing?"
[barely audible] "Looking for me!"

Fear is a strange thing in that it can make us hide from those who love us most and want to help us. The first mention of fear in the Bible is exactly like that, Adam and Eve hid from God because they were afraid. Ever since people have been trying to hide from the God who can heal their deepest pain and meet their greatest need.

Ann Landers was one of America's most famous newspaper counselors. She became the world's most widely read columnist and received on average 10,000 letters every month, almost all of them burdened with life's problems. When asked if there was one issue people suffered with more than any other she replied, "Fear."

In a report about fears titled *Trapped by a Web of Phobias,* the *Daily Mail* newspaper stated,

> "Britain is becoming a nation in fear, as dark terrors rise out of our subconscious and make an ever increasing number of people sit shuddering alone or locked away. More than 16 million of us apparently suffer from an anxiety disorder or phobia that affects our lives in some way. They can strike anyone, regardless of age or sex. There are more than 400 distinct phobias recognised by doctors. One internet site (www.phobialist.com) catalogues more than 1,000 phobias."

It went on to say,

> "There is also research which shows that the age at which anxiety strikes is coming down; 20 years ago most people who approached the Phobic Society were in their 40s or older, but now they are more likely to be younger."

A Harris Poll national survey of 4,000 adults and 1,600 children in the USA showed that 86 per cent of adults and 91 per cent of youngsters admitted to being "very afraid of something." Nearly one in five adults also said they are scared of more things now than they were as a child. The reason the most repeated command of Scripture is "fear not" (366 times) is because our world is full of fear.

Here's a list of some "celebrity" fears I came across,

* Orlando Bloom, star of *The Lord of the Rings* film trilogy, suffers from swinophobia, which is a fear of pigs.

* Alfred Hitchcock, the late great film director, was terrified of eggs and frightened of oval shapes such as balloons, (ovophobia).

* Billy Bob Thornton, Hollywood film star, has a fear of antique furniture.

* Julius Caesar may have conquered much of the known world and was revered as a god but never overcame his terror of thunder (astraphobia).

* Peter the Great of Russia cried like a child when he had to cross bridges.

* Hans Christian Anderson, the famous storywriter, had a phobia of being buried alive. As a result, he always carried a note in his pocket telling anyone who might find him unconscious not to assume he was dead. He often left another note on his bedside table stating, "I only seem dead."

Fear can make you do some bizarre things

* Dr Samuel Johnson, the celebrated British writer, refused to enter a room with his left foot first, if he did, he backed up and re–entered using his right one.

* Robert Trench was once the Episcopal Archbishop of Dublin, Ireland. He shared how for many years he was possessed by an unreasonable fear that one day he would lose all feeling in his legs and become paralyzed. He was constantly feeling his legs and pinching himself. One

evening while attending a large formal dinner, Trench reached under the table to pinch his leg, but he didn't feel anything. With an expression of shock he said aloud, "Oh, no! It's finally happened; I'm paralyzed. I can't feel my legs!" At that moment the dignified lady seated beside him fastened a cold gaze on him and said, "Reverend, would you kindly stop pinching my leg!"

Fear is the dark room in which negatives are developed

Fears will always cause us to live on the defensive because they have the power to make us look on the negative and never the positive. A fearful person becomes a pessimist and problem focused, life's challenges become more about what may go wrong than what can go right. The Israelites fought and won battles in the wilderness but did not enjoy the Promised Land.

We can also spend our whole life fighting and winning battles with anxiety and fear and at the same time be worn out and never enter what God has for us. A whole generation of Israelites died in the desert because they allowed fear to control them. We read ten of the spies sent to report on the Promised Land *"made the people's hearts melt with fear,"* Joshua 14:8. They said, *"We were like mere grasshoppers in our own eyes,"* Numbers 13:33. Fear will always magnify the enemy and the trials we face. It will grow in our minds and hearts until we believe its propaganda and give in to its despair. It attacks our belief of who we are in God and His promises to us. Its purpose is to get us to see the problems and challenges in comparison with our own limited resources instead of God's supernatural abundance. Two of the twelve spies, Joshua and Caleb, did eventually enter the Promised Land. They were not intimidated. They saw the same giants and fortified cities as the other ten but they looked at them in comparison to God. How we deal with fear determines our destiny.

Goliath taunted the armies of Israel and caused them to flee in terror. He was a warrior, a giant and a big mouth. All the Israelite soldiers could see was his huge stature and spear and all they could hear were his terrifying threats, *"When the Israelites saw the man, they all ran from him in great fear,"* 1 Samuel 17:24. When David saw and heard the same things it filled him with righteous anger and spiritual passion. He ran to fight Goliath saying,

> *You come against me with sword and spear and javelin, but I come against you in the name of the Lord Almighty, the God of the armies of Israel, whom you have defied.*
>
> 1 Samuel 17:45

The Israelite soldiers saw Goliath and thought he was too big to fight but David saw he was too big to miss.

Having a Fear and a Having a Fright

We all have frights from time to time. Sometimes we even enjoy them so we pay to watch a scary film or ride a fast rollercoaster. We sometimes laugh when someone is frightened and responds amusingly. Frights can also be beneficial and powerful motivators so that we learn to recognise and respond to danger wisely. When confronted by a ferocious dog or a wild animal our bodies respond by releasing adrenaline that increases the heart rate, heightens reaction time and supplies added strength to deal with the danger.

It reminds me of the young man whose job required him to work late in the evening. On his way home he found the shortest route was to walk through a cemetery near where he lived. One night he accidentally fell into a freshly dug grave. At first he was not too concerned, but when he realized he could not get out because the hole was too deep, he became somewhat hysterical. Finally, in complete exhaustion, he sat down in the corner of the grave and fell asleep. Shortly afterwards another man walking through the graveyard fell into the same grave. He too went through great effort to get out but couldn't. As he moved around the grave he stepped on the first person who woke up and shouted, "You can't get out of here!" But at that moment he did.

Having a fear is totally different from having a fright. Whereas a fright challenges a fear seeks to control. It desires to become part of who we are and shape and define us. This is why the problem with having a fear is that the fear ends up having some part of us. It affects our thinking, not just what we think but the way we have learned how to think.

When you have a fear it works at a subconscious level within you all the time. It causes that aspect of your life and thinking to be defensive and negative. When confronted by illness you are more likely to have developed a theology of sickness than belief in healing. When challenged by financial issues your thoughts are more controlled by poverty and greed than by contentment and generosity.

A fright is when challenged about your employment you respond wisely and work well. Like the man who was asked, "How long have you been working here?" He replied, "Ever since they threatened to fire me!" A fear is to live in dread of losing your job even when things are going well. A fright is when you look at the spending compared with your income and realise you need to cut back. A fear is that no matter how much you possess it is never enough and you find it hard to enjoy what you have. A fear of poverty is one which may have come through seeing your parents struggle financially or because you have gone through hard times. It may even be because of the 24 hour news we have today that not only reports news but also likes to make it, much of which is full of anxiety and fear about health and financial concerns.

The problem with many fears is that they become so much a part of how we feel and what we think we do not realise how much they define us and effect us. Unlike phobias which tend to be quite extreme and obvious, many fears live and hide under the surface stealing our joy, peace and faith. They drive us and drain us. They compel us and compromise us. They rob us and they rule us. At their root is the belief and feeling that something bad is going to happen to our health, our loved ones, our finances, our friendships, our jobs and our ministries and on it goes. We become unable to enjoy today because of what tomorrow may bring. It's like the man who said, "I always feel bad when I am good in case I feel bad tomorrow."

To try and deal with it we turn to such things as the power of positive thinking but all this does is cover it over. What we need most is to develop the principle of godly thinking.

Freedom from Fear

David said, *"I sought the Lord and He answered me, He delivered me from all my fears,"* Psalm 34:4. To live free from the destructive power of all fear we need to understand the three main areas in which it works.

1). There is a *State* of fear that comes upon us.

Job said, *"What I feared has come upon me; what I dreaded has happened to me,"* Job 3:25.

We therefore have to learn to **resolve** not to give in to fear however much we feel it.

Rosa Parks was a committed Christian and became mother of the Civil Rights movement in America at a time when racial segregation was enforced by law. She was arrested in 1955 for refusing to give up her seat on a bus to a white man. Boycotts and bloodshed followed until the Supreme Court finally ruled racial segregation unconstitutional.

In her book *Quiet Strength* she wrote,

> "Knowing what must be done does away with fear. When I sat down on the bus that day, I'd no idea history was being made – I was only thinking of getting home. But I had made up my mind. After many years of being a victim of the mistreatment my people suffered, not giving up my seat and whatever I had to face afterwards wasn't important. I didn't feel any fear...I felt the Lord would give me the strength to endure whatever I had to face. It was time for someone to stand up or in my case to sit down."

When you read through the Psalms you can't help but notice how often the psalmist exercises his will to overcome his emotions of fear,

> *When I am afraid, I **will** trust in you. In God, whose word I praise, in God I trust; I **will** not be afraid. What can mortal man do to me?*
>
> Psalm 56:3,4
>
> *God is our refuge and strength, an ever–present help in trouble. Therefore we **will** not fear, though*

*the earth give way and the mountains fall into the
heart of the sea.*

Psalm 46:1,2

2).   There is a ***Spirit*** of fear that comes against us.

"Elijah was afraid and ran for his life," 1 Kings 19:3.

We stand against this fear by learning to **rebuke** it.

I have a good friend who recently experienced an amazing healing. Three doctors and consultants told him he needed radical surgery for the large tumour that had showed up on X-rays and scans. Every test was positive and he needed a major operation. Such news can be devastating but he tells that the first thing he and his wife did when they sat in their car outside the hospital after being given the prognosis, was to pray stating their trust in God and rebuking the spirit of fear.

The next few weeks he was prayed for several times and he believed God had done an amazing healing in his body. When he went back to the hospital in West Wales for the planned operation he made the consultants promise that before they operated they would take one final scan to see if the cancer was still there. The registrar and consultant were not Christians but agreed reluctantly to his request. Miraculously every sign of the cancer had gone. The consultant surgeon wrote on my friend's medical report, of which he has a copy, that there was no trace of cancer and that the patient believes in the power of prayer.

3).   There is a ***System*** of fear that is all around us.

*"Men will faint from terror, apprehensive of what is
coming on the world,"* Luke 21:26.

It is our **relationship** with God that empowers us to overcome this.

Selwyn Hughes in his autobiography tells of the time when he was diagnosed with prostate cancer and the fear that accompanied it. He says that after 50 years of walking with the Lord his approach to dealing with the fear was simply to acknowledge it, bring it to an Almighty Sovereign God and allow His grace and love to deal with it.

It is our relationship with God that enables us to conquer and overcome the power of fear. It is allowing His amazing love to fill every area of our life. 1 John 4:18 tells us that, *"perfect love drives out fear."* Perfect love is not a power, a principle or a programme but a person, who loved us long before we loved Him, 1 John 4:10.

The problem many of us have is that while we believe God's love for us we find it difficult to receive His love in us, especially where fear has taken hold. We need to know how to allow the perfect love of God to come and *"drive out all fear."* I have learned that one very effective way of doing this is to face the fear and specifically apply God's love to it over and over again, sometimes by quoting scripture or listening to praise and worship and then declaring and receiving God's love into that specific fear and what has caused it. Being specific helps us to receive and target the root of the anxiety. Some fears are powerful strongholds which have been a part of us for a long time. If you had a sore neck you wouldn't put cream on your toe! In the same way we need to receive God's healing and freedom where it is needed.

The Apostle John also tells us,

> *But if anyone obeys his word, God's love is truly made **perfect** in him. This is how we know we are in him...Whoever loves his brother lives in the*

light, and there is nothing in him to make him stumble.

1 John 2:5,10

God's love is perfected in us not only as we grow in our love for God but also as we grow in love for others. For love to be perfected we have to learn not only to receive it but also to release it. The more we try and keep love to ourselves we lose it but the more we give away the more we have.

For many years, Joseph Tson was a pastor, teacher and evangelist in his native Romania. In 1972, he began to stand against governmental intrusion into the affairs of the church, insisting that Jesus alone was Lord over His church. He was immediately accused of "endangering the security of the state" and spent the next ten years being harassed, interrogated, and imprisoned by the Communist authorities. Finally, in 1981 he and his wife and daughter were permanently exiled from their homeland. Today he devotes much of his time to overseeing the translation, printing, and distributing of theological books for Christians in Romania.

He tells how God liberated him from the power of fear during his times of torture and persecution. In 1977 he was arrested for treason and told he would be shot. He says, "I just smiled and the interrogator asked why I smiled? I said I was not frightened for when you shoot me I will go to glory." He continues,

> "It was an amazing moment when I understood those who wanted to kill me were not my enemies. In 1974 I was under house arrest and I was interrogated every day for six months for the authorities to build up a case for trial but the real purpose was to break me. The man who interrogated me was the most wicked interrogator

in the system. I told him I prayed for him and shared about my life and ministry. There were always two of them because they didn't trust each other, but one day one of them went out and this man said to me, 'Let me tell you, whenever I interrogate people I feel how they hate me and I understand why, but with you it is different. It is a delight for me to be with you'." Tson concludes, "I was liberated from fear because I loved Him."

10

Overcoming the Spirit of Death

Death has been swallowed up in victory
1 Corinthians 15:54

My friend said, "She is dead." He was scared. I have never seen a man so frightened in my life. "What shall I do?" he asked. You may think that what I did was absurd, but I reached over into the bed and pulled her out. I carried her across the room, stood her against the wall and held her up, as she was absolutely dead. I looked into her face and said, "In the name of Jesus, I rebuke this death." From the crown of her head to the soles of her feet her whole body began to tremble. "In the name of Jesus, I command you to walk," I said. I repeated, "In the name of Jesus, in the name of Jesus, walk!" and she walked. Smith Wigglesworth recounts this amazing miracle in his book *Ever Increasing Faith.*

Death is everywhere in our world. Physical death, spiritual death, emotional death, mental death, social death, everywhere you go you will find it at work. Everything in our universe is dying. This is not some morbid pessimism but "a fact of life." The Bible says all creation is groaning wanted to be liberated from its bondage to decay (Romans 8:22), and scientists tell us the cosmos is "running down." The only thing that is not dying is our spirit within us that has been created to be eternal.

Understanding Death

Death is a place, a process and a power. There is a state of death (when our physical bodies die). There is a system of death which is the power of sickness, disease, despair, moral and spiritual darkness, depravity, destitution, violence, murder and so forth. There is also a spirit of death because death is not just a physical experience but also a demonic enemy and activity.

The Bible says that death is the last enemy to be destroyed, (1Corinthians 15:26). This is seen in the book of Revelation when, after the devil, the beast and the false prophet have already been thrown into the lake of fire,

> *Then death and Hades were thrown into the lake of fire.*
>
> Revelation 20:14

The expression *"Death and Hades"* occurs several times in the book of Revelation,

> *I looked, and there before me was a pale horse! Its rider was named **Death, and Hades** was following close behind him.*
>
> Revelation 6:8

> *The sea gave up the dead that were in it, and **Death and Hades** gave up the dead that were in them, and each person was judged according to what he had done.*
>
> Revelation 20:13

Death and Hades are mentioned together but they are distinct from each other. Death is personified as a spirit and Hades is the place (abode) of the dead.

Through His death and resurrection Jesus has all authority and power over the devil and death. Jesus not only rose from the dead but in doing so conquered the power of death. He said to the Apostle John on the Island of Patmos,

> *Do not be afraid. I am the First and the Last. I am the Living One; I was dead, and behold I am alive for ever and ever! And I hold the keys of **Death and Hades**.*

Revelation 1:18

When Jesus said, *"I tell you the truth, if anyone keeps my word, he will never see death,"* John 8:51, He angered and perplexed the Jewish leaders. They responded, *"Now we know that you are demon-possessed! Abraham died and so did the prophets, yet you say that if anyone keeps your word, he will never taste death,"* John 8:52. But Jesus did not say His followers will never experience death and physically die, He said they will never *see* "death" for even though they die they will not see death they will see life. He promised that even when some of them would be put to death on account of His name, not a hair of their heads would perish, Luke 21:16-18, John 11:25,26.

For those who love the Lord death is only a shadow, Psalm 23:4. For there to be a shadow there must be a light and the light is God's presence and protection,

> *Even though I walk through the valley of the shadow of death, I will fear no evil, for you are with me; your rod and your staff, they comfort me.*

Psalm 23:4

We read in Ecclesiastes 3:2,11, *"There is a time to be born and a time to die, and God has made everything beautiful in its time."* Death for a Christian is something to be faced not feared. In his November 2001 newsletter Dr James Dobson commented on the attack on the World Trade Centre, "I'm reminded of the young man who received an e-mail from his father, who worked in the World Trade Centre, on the day of the attacks. It simply read, 'I love you. I'll see you in heaven.'"

The Spirit of Death

When Elijah ran away from Jezebel's threats to kill him it was because a spirit of fear came upon him and a spirit of death came against him. Spewing out of her mouth came not only words but with them the unleashing of demonic powers and particularly the spirit and power of death. This helps to explain why Elijah, who had just won a great spiritual victory on Mount Carmel, runs and hides in the desert. As Jezebel lifted up her voice against him a spirit of death was unleashed. The effects this produced are very revealing, fear, anxiety, depression, discouragement, confusion, exhaustion, fatigue and wanting to die,

> *He came to a broom tree, sat down under it and prayed that he might die. "I have had enough, Lord," he said. "Take my life; I am no better than my ancestors."*
>
> 1 Kings 19:4

The devil does not have power to kill us but he does at times cause those like Jezebel to threaten our lives. He also seeks by a spirit of death to attack us in the same way as Elijah so that we think that life is not worth living.

The Spirit of Life

> *The thief comes only to steal and kill and destroy;*
> *I have come that they may have life, and have it to*
> *the full.*

John 10:10

The spirit of death not only attacks the quantity of our life to reduce it but also comes against the quality of our lives by bringing misery, sickness and despair. It is the opposite of the spirit of eternal life in Christ which is both a quality and quantity of living.

Part of Elijah's restoration process was to see that God was still sovereign and in control. More than 7000 had not *"bowed the knee"* to Jezebel and engaged in Baal worship. To overcome the spirit of death (and fear that always accompanies it) we need to understand and declare God's sovereign purposes over our life. Elijah was not going to leave this world in Jezebel's coffin but in God's chariot.

Theologians speak about the permissive will of God and the perfect will of God. Everything that happens God permits but that doesn't mean it is His perfect will. This is why we are told to pray for, *"His will to be done"* and for *"His kingdom to come on earth as it is in heaven."*

In Romans we are told to,

> *Offer your bodies as living sacrifices, holy and*
> *pleasing to God, this is your spiritual act of*
> *worship. Do not conform any longer to the*
> *pattern of this world, but be transformed by the*
> *renewing of your mind. Then you will be able to*
> *test and approve what God's will is, his **good,***
> ***pleasing and perfect will.***

Romans 12:1,2

111

We stand against the devil's will by submitting to and seeking to live in God's perfect will for our lives. Both John Calvin and John Wesley are reported to have said, "I am immortal until my work is done." When we seek to live in the perfect pleasing will of God for our lives we can also say "We are immortal until our work is done" and the best is still to come.

You will probably have heard it said, "We won't die before our time." But what does that mean? Our time can come because of something selfish or even stupid we have done or what others have done to us. I don't want to die in my time or in the devil's time but only in God's time. And neither do I want to come under the power of the spirit of death that eats away at the quality of my life. I therefore submit to God's perfect will and resist and rebuke the devil's purposes and plans.

They tried to kill Jesus by throwing Him off a cliff but He walked straight through the crowd unharmed, Luke 4:28-30. There was a death warrant put out on Him (Matthew 12:14, 26:4, Mark 3:6, 14:1, Luke 13:31, 19:47, John 5:18, 7:9, 25, 8:37, 40), yet Jesus knew He was secure in His Father's care.

> *The reason my Father loves me is that I lay down my life only to take it up again. No one takes it from me, but I lay it down of my own accord. I have authority to lay it down and authority to take it up again. This command I received from my Father.*
>
> John 10:17,18

> *I have brought you glory on earth by completing the work you gave me to do.*
>
> John 17:4

Jesus declared He was immortal until His work was completed and on the cross He cried, *"It is finished."*

The apostle Paul's life was threatened many times. He was stoned, beaten, imprisoned, tortured and left for dead. Shipwrecks and poisonous snakes had even tried to finish him off but nothing succeeded. God miraculously saved and restored him time after time. In the last letters he wrote to Timothy Paul says that he knows God's time for him to depart is soon to come. When he was in prison God had sent an earthquake (Acts 16), but this time the devil was sending an executioner. Yet Paul says it is not the devil or Nero who is in control of his life or his death. His times were in God's hands (Psalm 31:15),

> *I know whom I have believed, and am convinced that he is able to guard what I have entrusted to him for that day.*
>
> 2 Timothy 1:12

> *For I am already being poured out like a drink offering, and the time has come for my departure. I have fought the good fight, I have finished the race, I have kept the faith.*
>
> 2 Timothy 2:6-7

When the apostle Peter was in jail and facing execution (Acts 12) we read he was fast asleep. James had already been killed by Herod, so the church in Jerusalem was praying fervently for Peter's release. Years before Peter had been told by Jesus (John 21:18,19) the kind of death he would experience but it would not happen until he was an old man. Now in about his late thirties Peter could be confident that no matter how many guards he was chained to or how strong the prison doors God would rescue him. An angel was sent to set Peter free and *"rescued him from Herod's clutches and from everything the Jewish people were anticipating,"* Acts 12:11.

In the same conversation Peter had about his future with Jesus by the Sea of Tiberius in John 21, we are told that the apostle John was following them. When Peter asked what would happen to John, Jesus answered, *"If I want him to remain alive until I return, what is that to you? You must follow me."* We are told a rumour spread that John would not die but Jesus did not say that, only that whatever happened to others Peter must follow Jesus. What is interesting is that John did outlive all the other apostles and was the only one not to die a martyr's death. Tradition tells us that before he was sent to Patmos (a Roman prison colony) the Emperor Tiberius sentenced him to be executed by being boiled in oil. Miraculously he was unharmed so instead he was sent to the salt mines of Patmos. It was there he received the Revelation of Jesus and what was to come in the end times, which is the last book of the Bible. John's mission was not yet over and he was immortal until his work on earth was completed.

I do not pretend to understand all the mysteries of death and sickness, why good people die young and bad people live long. But I do know there is a great truth and power in declaring over our lives, our loved ones and our destiny the sovereign purposes of God. When we submit our lives to Him to live His perfect and pleasing will and pray for His kingdom to come we position ourselves to boldly and yet humbly say, "We are immortal until our work is done." We stand against the spirit of premature death.

This does not mean we can live and do as we please but we seek to live and do as God pleases. David says in Psalm 139 that God knows everything about us and adds, *"All the days ordained for me were written in your book before one of them came to be,"* (v16). May every day God has ordained for us come to pass and be filled with His *"goodness and mercy"* which He has promised will follow us all the days of our life, (Psalm 23).

Prayer

I declare that in you, Lord Jesus, death has no power over me and the spirit of death has no authority in my life. Therefore, I break the power of the fear of death and dying. I take authority over the spirits and powers of death that bring pain and misery. I declare that in Christ I am saved from death's powers not only when I die but also as I live.

Amen

11

The Ministry of Angels

Suddenly an angel of the Lord appeared and a light shone in the cell.
He struck Peter on the side and woke him up. "Quick, get up!" he
said, and the chains fell off Peter's wrists.

Acts 12:7

Billy Graham's best selling book *Angels* has sold over three million copies. In it he tells many fascinating accounts of angelic provision and protection. One such story is of the Rev John G Paton, pioneer missionary in the New Hebrides Island in the Pacific in the nineteenth century. Hostile natives surrounded his mission headquarters one night, intent on burning the Patons out of their home and killing them. John Paton and his wife prayed all through that terror filled night that God would deliver them. When daylight came they were amazed to see that unaccountably the attackers had left. They thanked God for saving them.

A year later, the chief of the tribe was converted to Jesus Christ, and Paton, remembering what happened that night asked the chief what had kept him and his men from burning down the house and killing them. The chief replied in surprise, "Who were all those men you had with you there?" The missionary answered, "There were no men just my wife and I." The chief argued that they had seen many men standing guard – hundreds of big men in shining garments with drawn swords in their hands. They seemed to circle the mission station so that the natives were afraid to attack. Only then did Paton realise how God had sent His angels to protect them. The chief agreed there was no other explanation.

Angels are mentioned in scripture over 300 times, both the Old and New Testament are full of their ministry and activity. For every one demon there are at least two angels, for we are told one third of the angelic host were cast out of heaven when they followed the devil in his rebellion, Revelation 12:4.

There was a time in Israel's history when the people of Jerusalem were once again in great danger. The Assyrian army had mobilized its vast war machine against the cities of Judah and conquered everything before it. Now the capital was surrounded and defeat and devastation was imminent. The Assyrian generals arrogantly told King Hezekiah that he and his people were doomed and no man or god would be able to come to their aid. When Hezekiah heard this he sent a message to Isaiah the prophet who replied, *"go and tell your master this is what the Lord says, 'Do not be afraid,'"* Isaiah 37:6.

When Hezekiah received another letter from the Assyrian commander warning him of the city's destruction he went into the Temple of the Lord and spread out the message before God and prayed. God spoke again through Isaiah telling the king that Assyrian troops would not enter the city because God Himself was defending it, (Isaiah 10–38).

Jerusalem did not fall. An angel of the Lord came and put to death 185,000 Assyrian warriors. Archaeologists excavating the site last century made the remarkable discovery of tens of thousands of skeletons buried in the sands outside Jerusalem.

In the book of Hebrews we are told angels are ministering spirits sent to serve those who will inherit salvation 1:14. Therefore angels are very active when it comes to spiritual warfare. Even though there are demonic powers against us there are even greater angelic forces for us. There is a fascinating insight into this in the life of Elisha when the King of Aram sent soldiers and chariots to take the prophet captive. When they arrived at Dothan where he was staying, Elisha's servant cried out in fear when he saw they had surrounded them,

"Don't be afraid," said Elisha, **"Those who are with us are more than those who are with them."** *And Elisha prayed, "O Lord, open his eyes so he may see." Then the Lord opened the servant's eyes, and he looked and saw the hills full of horses and chariots of fire all around Elisha.*

2 Kings 6:16,17

What is significant are the words *"Those who are* **with us** *are more than those who are* **with them**.*"* Elisha saw into the spiritual realm and could see there were more angelic powers protecting him than there were demonic forces with the soldiers sent to take him prisoner.

The angel of the Lord encamps around those who fear him, and he delivers them.

Psalm 34:7

For he will command his angels concerning you to guard you in all your ways.

Psalm 91:11

12

Meeting Trouble Triumphantly

The more a diamond is cut the brighter it sparkles

In 1984 the world's biggest tent was erected and dedicated in Soweto, South Africa, which was able to seat 34,000 people and was a miracle of God's provision. The first two week evangelistic crusade by Reinhard Bonke and the *Christ for all Nations* team saw 25,000 professions of faith to Christ and excitement was running high. A few months later preparations were well under way for the next crusade in Cape Town. The big tent had been put up on Cape Flats ready for the great outreach that was soon to commence. Vicious storms, however, battered the Cape and on May 6 just months after the tent's completion it was torn into a thousand pieces as if put through a paper shredder in a wild frenzy of destruction. The team members knelt and wept unashamedly. Millions of prayers and millions of dollars were swept away in hours by a wicked wind. Amazingly no one was injured but the question on almost everyone's lips was where would they go from here? Was this the end?

They had to make a decision on whether or not to continue the crusade and they decided they would. Then God did two miracles, the first was strangely regarding the weather. The rainy season had come, and the expected torrential rain would have ruined the open air crusade. When leaflets were handed out saying the crusade was going ahead many locals mocked predicting further humiliation and disaster. So Suzette Hatting, who led the prayer ministry, rose at 5am each morning to travel across town leading prayer meetings, praying for the weather. Yet as the crusade came closer it seemed to get worse, the storms that battered the Cape the week before the crusade were described as the worst in living memory. Yet on the day of the crusade's start the weather cleared up, even though a few miles away there was rain, day after day this miracle was reproduced. Warm air filtered in and for the next three weeks the Cape Peninsula basked in the most glorious sunny and warm weather, a fact that puzzled the weather experts who described it as an Indian summer.

Then came the second miracle as it soon became evident that those attending would never have fitted inside the 34,000 seater tent. By the end of the mission crowds of 75,000 were in attendance and thousands were converted. Since that time the ministry of *Christ for All Nations* has ministered to crowds of over two million in just one meeting, no tent could have ever been big enough.

In the following passage describing his ministry the apostle Paul uses the same word four times,

> *Praise be to the God and Father of our Lord Jesus Christ, the Father of compassion and the God of all **comfort**, who **comforts** us in all our troubles, so that we can **comfort** those in any trouble with the **comfort** we ourselves have received from God.*
>
> 2 Corinthians 1:3,4

The four fold repetition of the word *comfort* is a deliberate emphasis on his part. He speaks with the voice of personal experience and if ever a man had earned the right to speak on meeting trouble triumphantly he surely had. He lived no sheltered life. There had been shipwrecks and stoning, flogging and imprisonment, fierce persecution and opposition, the misunderstanding of friends and the diabolic activities of vindictive foes. Then there was all the pressure from the churches and those within them who criticised and condemned him. One commentator described Paul's trials and hardships by saying it reminded him of a bleeding rabbit running across a snow covered field. There was a trail of blood everywhere he went.

To understand what Paul is saying we need to know what he meant by the word *comfort*. It is not what we often associate with it such as having a comfortable lifestyle or an easy time.

The Greek word comfort, *"paraklesis"*, means, "calling in help." We get the word *paraklete* from the same root which speaks of the Holy Spirit as our Comforter. But again the meaning is not as some spiritual nanny but one who comes to aid and equip and empower us to overcome and stand strong no matter what is coming against us. When Paul speaks of being comforted he is talking about having his whole personality supernaturally reinforced. He is not talking about a lighter burden but rather a stronger back. Paul's confidence in the midst of all adversity was the source from which his "comfort" came. It was from God Himself, *the God of all comfort."*

When trouble comes there are natural resources and reserves we can draw upon and to a degree they will sustain us. Some look to science and technology, others psychology and some utopian optimism. Then there are those who escape into their materialism and hedonism while others cling to some religious belief or philosophy but ultimately all these are destined to fail.

Human cleverness and ability are no answer to the devil's cunning and adversity. Paul's strength was in God and so must ours be, for then we will be able to stand against and overcome all the devil's attacks.

With God we will gain the victory,
and he will trample down our enemies.

Psalm 108:13

Standing on God's Promises

The Lord watches over you, the Lord is your shade at your right hand; the sun will not harm you by day, nor the moon by night. The Lord will keep you from all harm, he will watch over your life; the Lord will watch over your coming and going both now and forevermore.

Psalm121:5-8

You will not fear the terror of night, nor the arrow that flies by day, nor the pestilence that stalks in the darkness, nor the plague that destroys at midday. A thousand may fall at your side, ten thousand at your right hand, but it will not come near you.

Psalm 91:5-7

No weapon forged against you will prevail, and you will refute every tongue that accuses you.

Isaiah   54:17

Who shall separate us from the love of Christ? Shall trouble or hardship or persecution or famine or nakedness or danger or sword? As it is written: "For your sake we face death all day long; we are considered as sheep to be slaughtered." No, in all these things we are more than conquerors through him who loved us.

Romans 8:35-37

I have given you authority to trample on snakes and scorpions and to overcome all the power of the enemy; nothing will harm you.

Luke 10:19

To him who is able to keep you from falling and to present you before his glorious presence without fault and with great joy to the only God our Saviour be glory, majesty, power and authority, through Jesus Christ our Lord, before all ages, now and forevermore! Amen.

Jude 24,25

They overcame him by the blood of the Lamb and by the word of their testimony.

Revelation   12:11

Books by David Holdaway

The Life of Jesus (More than half a million copies in circulation)

Winning Over Worry

The Life of Jesus More than A Prophet

They Saw Jesus

No More Fear

The Captured Heart

The Burning Heart

Never Enough

Surviving and Succeeding in a Financial Crisis

Was Jesus Rich?

Money and Spiritual Warfare

The Wonder of Christmas

Jesus the Wonder of Christmas

What Word Do All University Professors Spell Wrong?

How to Stand Against a Spiritual Attack